Also by Susie White

Second Nature: The Story of a Naturalist's Garden (2024)

"Deepens the reader's appreciation of their own garden." –*The Spectator*, year's best gardening books

"Honest and heartwarming." –*This England Magazine*

"A lyrical exploration of ... gardens and the natural world" –*WI Life*

"Lyrical, descriptive writing …a warm, companionable work" –*The English Garden*

"Touches your soul … a wonderful celebration of gardens and wildlife." –*The Reckless Gardener*

"A wonder of a book … filled with ideas, inspiration and advice … A special book that has transformative powers." –*Bramble Garden*

The Gardener and the Moth

IN THE MOMENT

Susie White

Saraband

Published by Saraband
3 Clairmont Gardens
Glasgow, G3 7LW
www.saraband.net

ISBN: 9781916812468

Note: Units of measure are given either in Imperial or Metric, depending on those best suited in each instance.

Printed and bound in Great Britain by Clays Ltd, Elcograf S.p.A.

1 2 3 4 5 6 7 8 9 10

Contents

For Lucy and Rory
and happy mornings spent
looking at moths

1

The Wonder of Moths and Butterflies

It's a June morning, a day of ease and sunshine, and my grandchildren have just arrived in an excited flurry. They're eager to watch me open the moth trap that I ran the night before and to experience the wonder of being close to these remarkable insects. In the night, the bright bulb was a beacon to draw moths down into a deep tub lined with egg boxes where they could settle and hide, ready for study by day. Now we'll discover what was flying in the night while we were asleep. If you've ever left on an outdoor light and seen moths fluttering around it or settling on a wall, you'll know how attracted they are to a source of light.

We cluster around the trap as I slowly remove the blanket that it was covered with to stop the moths escaping. This is the moment when you never know what you will find. That feeling of expectation never leaves me, no matter how many times I've repeated this. It's a treasure hunt, a bit of magic, and I become childlike in that moment too.

June is the perfect time to show moths to the children because I'm almost guaranteed to find hawk-moths. Slow-moving and spectacular in their shape and colour, they will rest on a finger if you're calm, unwilling to expend the energy it takes to lift their large bodies in flight.

My granddaughter holds a Poplar Hawk-moth in cupped hands, smiling in delight and concentration. The grey moth, with its sculpted wings, fills the whole of her five-year-old palm. My younger grandson gazes down at a second hawk-moth that is like a pinned brooch on the pocket of his red T-shirt.

Each egg box that I slowly extract from the large black tub holds a surprise. There's a sulphur yellow Brimstone Moth, its wings edged in chestnut brown triangles. A Coxcomb Prominent with its tufted punk headpiece. Garden Pebble, Green Carpet, Flame Shoulder and Latticed Heath, each with their own unique character and patterning. And the exotic pink and lime green of an Elephant Hawk-moth. These are moments of calm before the children run off along the garden paths, disturbing butterflies as they go.

Coming here to see the moths has become an early summer ritual as each year they grow older. I'm happy that I've been able to give them this experience, of this closeness to nature. Slow worms slipping between the layers of the compost heap, a bulky toad living under a tin sheet, water snails in the pond: these are all meetings in this wildlife garden that will stay with them. Nights when they've camped on the lawn, the children, their dad and the dog somehow getting some sleep in the tent after an excited dusk watching bats swoop and dive over our heads on the hunt for moths and other insects.

Moths and butterflies are just one aspect of this holistic garden, but a vital part of its ecosystem. I live in a tucked away valley in the North Pennines, a quiet part of Northumberland, the most sparsely populated county in England. It's a place of dark skies, clear air and wide landscapes. When I came here with my husband, David, fifteen years ago, the rubble and rubbish-strewn land around the house was no place for wildlife. I described how we made this bountiful garden from scratch in *Second Nature: The Story of a Naturalist's Garden*. And it is the insects that form one of the first layers that help it to function as a living garden, providing food for not only birds and bats but also mammals, spiders, other insects and amphibians.

Let me describe where I live. Our house nestles in the valley, reached by a long off-road track, so there's little to disturb the wildlife. It becomes a frost hollow in winter, a sun trap in summer, so plants have to be resilient to cope with these extremes of temperature. We've recorded a swing of 50°C between the coldest and hottest days. If you choose carefully and experiment with planting, I believe you can make a garden anywhere, especially if you include the native plants that grow around about.

The old house sits well in the landscape, its stone walls and roofs quarried locally or taken from the nearby river. With a burn running down one side and the main river on the other, there is a constant sound of water. To the front is the large flower garden, to the rear the vegetable garden, both bounded by drystone walls, many of which needed rebuilding by David when we first moved here. We'd been attracted by the derelict state of the land, a blank canvas in which to let loose the many plants I'd brought with me from my previous garden.

Now, fifteen years later, it has settled into a maturity that speaks of age and time, and matches the soft stone of the house. Topiary that began as found seedlings has evolved with yearly clipping into mounds of yew or domes of box, calm static points around which rises and falls the seasonal flow of the garden. This is slow gardening, and I have a different connection to these topiary shapes than if they had been bought fully grown from the garden centre.

There are only two cross paths to the flower garden and this allows for huge borders of unbroken planting, sanctuary for many forms of wildlife. Hedgehogs have overwintered beneath the thatched cover of ornamental grasses. Mallards have nested in the thickets of planting, as have red-legged partridges. Garden warblers have woven their nests between stems of comfrey, and voles scurry along retaining walls.

The ground, which when we moved here was lifeless and worm-less, is now packed with life from an annual mulching of the borders and the compost from our three bins that is laid over the vegetable garden. Leaf mould, gathered from the paths and the terraces, is distributed on the shady border beneath a line of sycamores, and fungi is abundant from the laying of wood chip. Each autumn erupts in the ice cream cone shapes of shaggy inkcaps that thrust through the borders or the paths. All this richness has come from ground that was bulldozed, compacted and dead.

The first thing that we did when we moved here was to build the compost bins and to recycle cardboard packing cases, lawn clippings, spent hops from the local brewery, anything that we could lay our hands on. The priority was the soil. Get life into that and everything else starts to shift and move. Brandling worms in fresh compost, bacteria and fungi, ground beetles, woodlice and springtails, there is now so much activity going on.

The next stage was to plant up the flower garden using species attractive to insects. This is the fundamental building block of an interconnected garden.

Having gardened professionally for many years, twenty-three of those spent managing a walled herb garden and nursery, I'd learned from observation and was able to bring a wealth of plant material with me. Growing from seed, especially annuals, added to the mix, but always with an emphasis on useful plants, those with accessible nectar or pollen, or with leaves for caterpillars.

It is in the combination of many different flower forms and shapes that we can attract a wide range of insects. That also makes it beautiful to the eye and, for me, a wildlife garden needs to please both the gardener and all the other beings that live in it. If you just let a garden go, certain species will quickly dominate and there will be a lack of diversity, which will then narrow down the life within it. I want to look out of the window and enjoy what I see, summer or winter, but also to know that I've provided shelter and food, that this is a space for all of us.

Some choices were easy. I had a mass of sedums so I used these to line the central path on either side, an autumn feast for bees and butterflies. The path that crosses it has repeated shapes of catmint, the large *Nepeta* 'Six Hills Giant', peonies and alliums. When I walk along this path, it is bustling with honeybees from a local hive, bumblebees and, in a grey blur of wings, the immigrant moth, the Silver Y.

Butterflies are universally appreciated and associated as being part of a wildlife garden. They are used as symbols on packaging to imply an eco-conscious product. They inspire jewellery, fabrics, art. Moths are often misrepresented, especially in the press where articles on clothes moths are inaccurately illustrated with harmless moths. Once you open your eyes to the incredible variety and beauty of these day- and night-flying insects, it really adds to your appreciation of the natural world.

A few years after moving here, I started to really notice the moths that were being attracted to the garden. Luckily, this coincided with a programme called Cold Blooded and Spineless that was being run by the North Pennines Area of Outstanding Natural Beauty (now a National Landscape). The aim was to celebrate and record the invertebrates of this upland area and, by gathering data, to better understand how to conserve them. A moth course was arranged in a local village hall to be run by leading authority Dave Grundy, who had set up the Garden Moth Scheme.

Dave came up from Birmingham and a group of us gathered in the fridge-like hall, the electric heaters above our heads being totally ineffective. I was cold for two days, made worse by it being the sunniest day outside on a Saturday for weeks! But it was a fantastic weekend course and it began my fascination with moths. We had to work hard. Dave showed us specimens but he would not tell us what they were, so we had to go through the various groups of species using field guides and work it out for ourselves. How much more I learned than if I had simply used an app to tell me what a moth was called.

That Saturday night, Dave came to our house and set up six light traps. He used two different types and the garden was lit by the blue glow of actinic traps beneath bird cherry, by long grass, in the borders, and also by the cold pinkish light of Robinson traps on the paved terrace and by the river. A curious hedgehog investigated the equipment unperturbed, tawny owls called in the trees, bats emerged from under the house roof, and a woodcock squeaked like a mouse as it flew over, just as Dave left to stay the night at the pub.

He came back at six o'clock in the morning to check on the haul. I've never been very good at getting out of bed early and dedicated 'mothers' often stay up through the night. Instead, I rely on my husband, David, who turns off the trap and covers it with a blanket until I have got up! For ten years now, I've been setting a Robinson trap once a week and submitting the data to the Garden Moth Scheme. It's the accumulation of information that helps to see patterns emerging and to know how healthy the insect population is.

There are around 2,500 species of moths in the UK and fifty-nine species of butterflies. That's fifty-seven residence species of butterflies plus two regular migrants, the Painted Lady and the Clouded Yellow. As the climate warms, insects become established in new places, die out or decline, so these numbers are in a state of flux. The moths are split into two groups: around 900 are the larger macro-moths, while the rest are micro-moths, some of which are very tiny. Both moths and butterflies are particularly threatened, so it's important to do anything that we can to help them within our gardens. They are like the canary in the coal mine, indicators of the health of the environment, and their loss impacts on so many other forms of life.

A year later, I went on a second course with Dave down in Teesdale, an area of wild upland moors and hay meadows. Shifting just thirty miles south from my home meant finding many similarities but also some different moths, a useful illustration of how regional many species are. It's the same with butterflies. The national picture comes from data submitted to the Garden Moth Scheme, the National Moth Recording Scheme and The UK Butterfly Monitoring Scheme from recorders living as far apart as John o' Groats and the Channel Islands.

My garden is just a small part of this but above all, it gives me pleasure. I have a favourite corner where I can sit on a wooden bench surrounded by plants growing in gravel. Scented marjoram and dianthus, blue vipers bugloss and silver sea holly, globes of alliums and soft textured lambs' ears, all plants that look beautiful and are busy with insects. Butterflies visit these plants by day, plants that are all chosen for their usefulness. The air is full of movement: the blur of wings, the sound of foraging bees and light shining through petals. At dusk, it becomes luminous with evening primrose, pale flowers glowing in the half-light and drawing moths to feed on their nectar. Day and night, this is a garden that is truly alive.

2
Butterfly or Moth?

During the 2024 Big Butterfly Count, organised annually by Butterfly Conservation, the top six species recorded were Gatekeeper, Meadow Brown, Large White, Small White, Peacock and Red Admiral. They were followed by Ringlet, Speckled Wood, Comma and Green-veined White. Some day-flying moths were on the list, but the rest of the butterflies that make up the top twenty-one records were Marbled White, Small Copper, Small Tortoiseshell, Common Blue, Brimstone, Holly Blue and Scotch Argus.

The butterflies that I'm writing about in this book are those that are most likely to visit our gardens. If you want to see others, you will probably need to visit a nature reserve or specialised landscape where they can be found. Of the fifty-nine

British butterflies, some are found in only specific locations. When it comes to moths, their species are so numerous that I can only describe some of them, but I'm writing about a wide variety as they are just so intriguing.

Learning to tell the difference

As a child, I was captivated by butterflies. I would stand gazing up at the tall purple asters that grew at the back of my parents' flower border and try to photograph them with my Instamatic camera. Weeks later, a paper envelope would come back from the shop, the printed pictures holding nothing of the magic that I'd seen. It was the experience, the being in the moment, that was magical.

I still feel a need to fix these elusive fleeting times in an image, partly to record what I see, but also to communicate this wonder to other people. I often need to remind myself to simply look. To be completely there without trying to capture anything. It's the same with naming. We categorise and pin down like those early naturalists – collecting lists and names that are necessary for understanding. So I have an ambiguous feeling towards my accumulation of data. As a naturalist, it's an important part of recording what I see. As an artist, it can sometimes get in the way of the direct and simple appreciation of the natural world.

Yet many of the names of these insects are evocative and descriptive, imaginative or quirky, so that they add something to my appreciation. It's wonderful to know that the marbled green and white patterning of a moth that looks like lichen is called Merveille du Jour, or that Mother Shipton is named after a Yorkshire witch. When I see the beautiful orange-brown Comma butterfly, I look for the white mark on its closed wing that gives it its name. These are things that add another dimension to these captivating insects.

Learning the difference between moths and butterflies is not always straightforward. Insects have evolved to fit the habitats they live in and the niches that they occupy in the ecosystem. Some have developed bright colours to confuse predators. Others are the opposite and are camouflaged to blend in with a background of grasses or bark. As a result, a butterfly might be dull in colour and a moth dramatic and vibrant. Telling the difference between them opens our eyes to so much variety and wonder.

The Ringlet is a quiet, muted butterfly that bobs along in flight on dull days among tall grasses and verges. A Six-spot Burnet moth, *Zygaena filipendulae*, sports crimson spots on black wings, flashes of vivid colour among meadows or by the sea. Yet because both fly by day, the moth is often mistaken for a butterfly. Its colourful patterns advertise its unpleasant taste and mild toxicity to birds. The butterfly blends with its surroundings, the moth flashes its message. Both are attempting to avoid being eaten.

Butterflies are generally active in the daytime, though the Red Admiral will fly at night when on migration. Moths can be on the wing by night or by day, so that's not a guide to which is which either. The keys to look for are in their bodily structure. The antennae of butterflies are long and thin with a club-like end, while moth antennae are feathery or thread-like. Some male moths have magnificent antennae, shaped like combs so the larger surface area can detect females from a long distance. No UK butterflies have feathered antennae but just to confuse things, those of the Six-spot Burnet moth smoothly taper to an elongated clubbed end!

Another clue is in their resting positions. Butterflies hold their wings vertically over their backs, brought together like hands in prayer. Moths generally rest with their wings spread out, as in the hawk-moths, or folded over their bodies. Again, there are exceptions, so the thorn moths, for example, hold their wings upright when they are still. In some species of moth, the females don't have any wings. They wait, flightless but giving out pheromones, until a male finds them.

Butterflies have slender, smooth bodies while the bodies of moths are generally thicker and hairy. The December Moth, *Poecilocampa populi,* is so fluffy that it looks as if it is wearing a shaggy hat to keep off the cold. And there's a difference in their lifecycles. When butterflies transform, they form a chrysalis that is generally smooth and hard, whereas moths spin a cocoon.

After a while, you learn what to expect. Both moths and butterflies have recognised flight periods or are associated with particular plants. You wouldn't expect to see a December Moth in summer or an Orange-tip butterfly in January. Size isn't a clue either because some moths are larger than butterflies. Moths have an incredible size range from the very tiny to impressively large. Both are important pollinators.

Moths developed first, and technically all butterflies are moths. They all belong to the order Lepidoptera, a name that means 'scaly-winged' and refers to the many dust-like scales that cover their wings. Within this order, they are divided into family, subfamily and species. Family might be, for example, the Geometridae or the Noctuidae, the two largest families of macro-moths in the UK. Narrowing it down further, in the Geometridae family you might find one of the Geometrinae, the emerald moths. And within that, a Large Emerald,

Geometra papilionaria, a commonly found and beautiful large green moth. I have a photograph of a friend who came to visit, an expression of delight on her face, as she gazes at a Large Emerald poised on the tip of her finger.

There are common names for groups of Lepidoptera; some of these are tiger moths, hawk-moths, skippers, butterflies, clearwing moths and plume moths. It can all seem a little overwhelming to begin with, the pages in a field guide lined with confusing ranks of similar looking moths, but once you get your eye in, it becomes easier to know what you are looking at. Butterflies are easier to distinguish and there are far fewer of them!

Identifying species

Mobile phones have made recording and identification much easier, a quick way of taking a photograph of a restless insect. You can do a reverse image search online and, although this doesn't always give the right answer, it can help to nudge you in the right direction. You can then check to see if the species you're looking at is likely to be in that habitat or flying at that time of year. It is, though, so much more rewarding to learn from the more time-consuming method of looking in a good field guide, and there's a recommended list at the back of this book.

As a child, I learned to identify wildflowers through my mother's copy of *The Concise British Flora*, a book of exquisite paintings made over a period of sixty years by the Rev Keble Martin. Each page is beautifully laid out with accurate watercolours that also express the feeling, the jizz in birding terms, of each flower. Looking at these helped me to recognise the links between different wildflowers, to realise that oregano, mint and thyme were all related because they are illustrated on the same page. In the same way, a field guide to moths or butterflies helps you to understand the relationships between the different species, something you don't get from a quick reverse image search.

Because I'm collecting data for a national scheme, it's important to be accurate, and there's plenty of help with identification. Facebook groups, both nationally and locally, give interaction and support, and there are some very knowledgeable people among them. Then there are online community groups such as iSpot and iNaturalist where you can post a picture along with a description of where you have seen an insect – or fungus, worm, bird or mammal – and replies are usually very quick.

For years, I've kept diaries, and these are a fascinating way to look back and re-experience what I've seen. They fill out an observation with descriptions and enhance the dry Excel spreadsheets. I underline a sighting because I have found it, making it easier to find among pages of handwritten notes. 'First Comma on campion flower', 'blackbird sunbathing on the stone wall', or 'curlews calling as they fly over our house'. And I keep a definitive list of moth and butterfly species, each one that I've seen in this garden, so that I know if there's something new. When people post on Facebook, they use the abbreviations NFH and NFY, for 'new for here' and 'new for year'.

There's also an app that I find very useful in identifying moths. Called *What's Flying Tonight?*, it draws on the records of volunteers that have been gathered through Butterfly Conservation's National Moth Recording Scheme. You can manually give a location, or it can use GPS to establish where you are, and it gives a photographic list of moths that are likely to be flying on that particular date. In addition, some counties (Hampshire, Devon and East Anglia, for example, are well covered) have their own websites showing what is likely to be flying tonight. By combining all these different methods – books, apps, local groups and your own records – you can create a picture of what is flying in your own garden, day and night.

Butterflies are generally easier to identify because there are a fewer of them and some are specific to certain locations so they are unlikely to visit gardens. The gorgeous Adonis Blue, *Polyommatus bellargus* – males have dazzling azure wings – is only found in southern England, has a unique life-cycle in combination with ants, and feeds solely on horseshoe vetch. The Duke of Burgundy, *Hamearis lucina*, prettily patterned in orange and brown, is a rarity found on chalk and limestone grasslands.

You're much more likely to have garden butterflies to your borders, the frequently seen species such as Small Tortoiseshell. These are the beauties that I remember from my childhood, though not all butterflies pleased my parents, who were trying to grow flowers and vegetables. I had my own small patch of garden; one of the best ways of getting children interested in nature is to give them autonomy over their own bit of soil. Here, I grew a mass of colourful peppery-leaved nasturtiums, and was fascinated to watch them being shredded by the striped caterpillars of Large White butterflies, *Pieris brassicae* – the key as to why gardeners are not so keen on them is in the name.

Those tall asters with their starburst amethyst flowers were dizzying with vibrant Red Admirals, Small Tortoiseshells and Peacocks. The occasional Brimstone, lime-yellow wings shaped like leaves, would flit through the borders, and autumn would be lively with beautiful scalloped-winged Commas. I was then much less aware of moths, outside lights being turned on after my bedtime, and it is now a great richness to be living among and gardening for both these enchanting insects.

Confusing whites

There are several white butterflies in the UK, four of which are very common, and are frequently seen in gardens. They are often dismissed and lumped together as cabbage whites but they are all valuable pollinators. They can be a bit difficult to distinguish when they're flying, but much easier when they're at rest. A male Orange-tip butterfly, *Anthocharis cardamines*, flaunts his day-glow colour on the ends of his wings, but the female is much quieter. She has black wingtips like some of the other white butterflies, which could be confusing, but look at the underside when a female has her wings closed as she feeds on a cuckoo flower: they have beautiful blotched markings in mossy green. An old name for this harbinger of spring is the rather charming 'lady of the woods'. The male also has this marbling on his closed wings.

Green-veined White butterflies, *Pieris napi*, are also best identified when their wings are closed. That's when you can see the pretty greeny-grey lines that radiate out from the body along its veins. The female lays her eggs on native plants such as hedge garlic and cuckooflower – the same species that the Orange-tip uses – and not on cultivated vegetables. The butterfly it could most likely be confused with is the Small White, *Pieris rapae*, but this doesn't have those prettily marked wings. Eggs are laid on the underside of brassica leaves and nasturtiums, and in fields of oil seed rape. So this, and the Large White, can be properly thought of as cabbage whites because of their food plants.

The population of Small White butterflies is added to by migrants from Europe every year. They are particularly attracted to yellow and white flowers, feeding on the nectar. There's a black corner marking on each forewing as well as a black dot. The Large White, *Pieris brassicae* (note the specific name!), is an altogether larger butterfly, also with black wingtips and with double dots on its forewings, and is a stronger looking insect. There's a very pretty subtle greeny-yellow colouring that you can see when its wings are closed. Those then are the common white butterflies, the others being scarce or unlikely to visit gardens.

Imaginative names

Early naturalists, from the Georgian era and later the Victorians, were fascinated by insects, as they were by so many things in the natural world. They categorised and collected, lining up labelled specimens in drawered cabinets. A fashion, a hobby, an obsession, it was also educational and has left us with valuable museum examples that can be studied and compared to the present day. These naturalists gave names to moths that were a mix of the imaginative and the prosaic, often reflecting the lifestyle of the people studying them. Their homes were furnished in wainscots and brocades, and they were waited on by footmen and lackeys.

The very words conjure up images: Peach Blossom, Brindled Beauty, Cinnabar, Rosy Rustic, Cream-spot Tiger. Some can make you yearn to see them. I'm probably never going to see a Clifden Nonpareil, a large moth with a flash of kingfisher blue on its underwings – its name means 'beyond compare' – but the exotic name just adds to its unattainability and allure.

A particularly endearing moth is enhanced by its descriptive name: the Spectacle, *Abrostola tripartita,* has a furry thorax which culminates near the head in a tufty Mohican. Look down on it from above and it's decorated in a pattern of browns with black central lines running across it, but when you turn it head-on, it looks like it's wearing a pair of spectacles. It's a fun one to share with children. There's something cartoonish about the white rings just above its eyes and no matter how many times I see it, Spectacle makes me smile.

Many names are lyrical associations. The Miller looks like it's dusted in flour. Puss Moth is furred like a tabby cat. White Ermine sports regal clothing. Blood-vein has a crimson slash running across its wings. The Ghost Moth, *Hepialus humuli*, is sexually dimorphic, the females being a blend of orange and apricot colouring while the males are white. In their courtship displays, they hover over grassland at dusk on warm evenings, alternatively flashing white wings and grey undersides so that they appear and disappear in a ghostly way.

This incredible gamut of designs and markings also led to many moths being given straightforwardly descriptive names. There's Figure of Eight, Heart and Dart, Green Silver-lines, Grey Arches and the day-flying Silver Y, named after the white shape on the outer wing. Others are more down to earth as in Square-spot, Clay and Reddish Buff. Because they don't conjure up quite the same images as Ghost Moth or Puss, they are not quite as memorable, and it's easy to confuse Bright-line Brown-eye with Brown-line Bright-eye! So those names can be very helpful in identifying at least some of the species. They seemed to have run out of ideas when it came to Suspected, Neglected, Confused and Uncertain!

Some moths are named after the plants that their caterpillars feed on, such as Mullein, Campion, Lychnis, Turnip and Foxglove Pug. Some are linked to the time of year that they emerge: March Moth, December Moth, November Moth and Winter Moth. Sometimes it's the caterpillars that evoked the name. The adult Elephant Hawk-moth that is often drawn to moth traps has wings that are a dazzling combination of pink and lime green, yet its caterpillar is the opposite of glamorous being a chunky grey-brown, the colour of an elephant's trunk. It clambers up the stems of willowherbs and, when alarmed, the enormous black eye spots on its head swell up to scare off predators. At the opposite end of the scale, most micro-moths are known only by their scientific names which, coupled with their small size and their similarities, makes them harder to identify.

Pest species

In my enthusiasm for these beautiful insects, I've not mentioned the comparatively small number of troublesome moths. An indoor infestation can be serious, threatening historic fabrics in stately homes and museums, making holes in natural fibres such as wool, or eating carpets. When I was shown around the collection stores of the Great North Museum in Newcastle upon Tyne, I was told what a problem this could be for taxidermy. It's the larvae that do the damage, and they feed on animal-based fibres such as feathers, wool and fur. They don't go for cotton, so your T-shirts are all right, or for man-made fibres such as nylon. There are several damaging species: Clothes Moth, Brown House-moth, White Shouldered House-moth and Tapestry Moth.

A couple of years ago, I was staying with a friend in London who had a big problem with Clothes Moths in his spare room. He assumed that anything that you could buy online would be safe and had distributed a whole bag of mothballs in cupboards, under towels and throughout wardrobes. As soon as I walked into the room, there was an overwhelming smell of naphthalene. This is obtained from coal tar, the liquid byproduct of the distillation of coal into coke for use as a smokeless fuel. Breathing in the fumes can affect your health, and the UK government website says that it was used as a fumigant for repelling moths in the past but this use is discontinued. However, an online search shows plenty are still for sale. We searched out every last mothball and bagged them up, and threw open the windows so that I could spend the night there.

Alternative treatments are to put small clothes in a freezer for at least two weeks, to store clean clothes long-term in vacuum-sealed bags, and to use natural repellents such as cedar balls or lavender to deter adult moths, though this will have no effect on larvae. There is also biological control: you can buy sachets of tiny parasitic wasps, *Trichogramma*, that will parasitise moth eggs, and there are now sticky pheromone traps for sale.

With climate change and world trade, new problems keep emerging. The Oak Processionary moth was brought in through the horticultural trade and is expanding from the south-east of England, doing serious damage to oak trees. The Box moth, *Cydalima perspectalis*, was imported from Southeast Asia and is adding to the problems of topiary and hedges created by the fungal disease box blight, so some gardeners are planting alternatives. Yet it's different when species have evolved together. Every year, a tree in our vegetable garden is covered in the larvae of the UK native Bird-cherry Ermine moth, *Yponomeuta evonymella*. It's an extraordinary sight, the caterpillars weaving protective webs around themselves, encasing leaves, twigs and branches, and in some years, the entire trunk. It runs in boom and bust cycles like so many natural events, and a recent year saw the whole tree looking ghostly, the trunk wrapped as if it was in a silk stocking. Even the table and chairs beneath the tree had been wrapped! When this happens, the tree is defoliated, but it is only for that season. I will find hundreds of Bird-cherry Ermine moths in the light trap and on the walls around it, small white moths with rows of little black dots on their wings. By the end of summer, the tree has recovered, grown new leaves and is none the worse for it.

3

Anatomy and Lifecycles

Life-cycle of moths and butterflies

Their anatomy

Butterflies and moths have three parts to their bodies, as do other insects. These are head, thorax and abdomen. They have two pairs of wings and six jointed legs (spiders, which are arachnids, have eight). The head has two compound eyes, a pair of antennae and a proboscis, which is used for feeding. This can be uncoiled deep into the throat of a flower and then curled back up like a spring. It's fascinating to watch a butterfly feeding, extending its proboscis like a drinking straw before neatly rolling it up again and moving to the next flower. Their eyes can detect light, colour and movement, and the antennae are used to pick up traces of chemicals in the air in order to find food or a mate. The thorax is where the wings and legs are attached, and the abdomen contains the digestive system and reproductive organs. This is where the eggs will develop in a female, and she lays them from the tip of her body. There are also tiny holes called spiracles down the sides of the abdomen, which are for breathing.

Most Lepidoptera have a similar lifestyle with tiny eggs being laid on the host food plant, although Swift moths scatter their eggs randomly while flying. Sometimes eggs are laid in clusters, sometimes singly. The female Orange-tip butterfly only lays one egg to a single flower head because the caterpillars are cannibalistic and may eat each other. She leaves traces of a pheromone as a sign to other females so that they won't lay on that particular flower stalk. Each egg from each species is a different shape and colour, pale yellow to green or orange, exquisite little gems that are worth searching out and looking at in detail with a hand lens.

The eggs laid by an adult hatch into caterpillars (larvae), which, after consuming their own egg, feed ravenously, gaining weight. They have soft bodies, which is what makes them easy and succulent prey for birds. As they eat voraciously, they change their skin to allow for the increase in size, and they do this by moulting four or five times as they grow. Each of these growth stages is called an instar and usually lasts for a few weeks. The larva then forms a pupa (chrysalis), a protective covering to allow for the next stage. This pupa might be underground or in leaf litter, attached to a plant stem and camouflaged to its surroundings, or fashioned in a silk cocoon. From this, the adult will emerge. It's while inside the pupa that the body of the insect goes through an incredible reorganisation to form the adult moth or butterfly. It breaks out of the pupa and, on first emerging, its wings are soft and crumpled, but they are pumped up with fluids and harden within about an hour. It's then off into flight, looking for another moth or butterfly to mate with.

Male moths have an incredible sense of smell, often aided by elaborate antennae, and follow the trail looking for a female. Females generally don't move far from their larval food plants, so they give off pheromones to attract the males, which are much more mobile. Not all moths drink nectar but many do, and this is where you can plan your garden as a banquet for insects. Nectar is a sugary liquid and the main energy source for adult pollinators. It's important for powering their flight muscles and giving them the energy to fly and find a mate. Or it might help to refuel after winter hibernation or after a long journey to Britain from Europe or Africa. Painted Lady butterflies, *Vanessa cardui,* make spectacular migrations from sub-Saharan Africa to Europe, a distance of 15,000km and played out over several generations. It's the longest round-trip made by any butterfly.

The Goat Moth, *Cossus cossus*, is our heaviest moth, its silver wings with their wavy black and grey parallel lines disguising it as a piece of bark. It has the longest larval stage of any UK moth, overwintering for three or four years as a larva, burrowing in and eating the wood of deciduous trees such as birch, alder, oak or apple. The caterpillars are supposed to give off a strong smell of male goat, hence its name, but being a scarce species, I've not had the opportunity to test this out! The sap run that leaks out of the hole made by Goat Moth larvae attracts other insects: nocturnal moths, hoverflies and Red Admiral butterflies.

Moths vibrate their wings to warm up their muscles before they can fly away and the heavier the body, the longer it takes. That's why hawk-moths are such great species to show to children: they will sit for a long time on your finger, reluctant to move unless feeling threatened. Then it's with quite an effort that they prepare for take-off, vibrating their wings at high speed (this is known as shivering) to increase their muscle temperature. The colder the day, the longer it takes. Because they have to expend so much energy doing this, it's kind, once you've studied them, to tuck them underneath foliage where they are protected from birds. Large Yellow Underwings, the bullies of the moth trap, don't seem to have this problem, and they just leap into the air, taking off with no preamble. And the tiny micro-moths that you find in meadows fly up in a flurry as you approach before settling back again, hidden among grass stems.

Diversionary tactics

It's well known that bats use echolocation when hunting, emitting high-pitched sounds and listening to the noise that bounces back from the objects around them. It's less well known that some moths have developed countermeasures. Some have evolved ultrasound-sensitive ears that can detect the squeaks of bats to avoid being caught. Others have ways of suddenly changing direction or doing loop the loop, while others emit their own high frequency noise to tell bats that they are toxic. Some genuinely are toxic while others are pretending to be to trick the bats into not eating them.

The rear of a male hawk-moth has stridulatory scales on the abdomen that it can rub, rather as grasshoppers do, in order to generate ultrasound. This confuses the bats, effectively jamming their sonar, so that they can't detect the moths. It's all part of the endless battle of survival skills between prey and predator.

Hiding in plain sight

Moths and butterflies have evolved amazing camouflage in order to protect themselves from predators.

These strategies enable them to blend into the background, but have also created the most extraordinarily complex and intriguing mimicry. The Buff-Tip, *Phalera bucephala*, is a night-flying moth that is attracted to light, luckily so as it gives us a chance to marvel at it. The wings are held vertically, mottled silver-grey, and have a rolled-up appearance like a fragment of silver birch. Its squared-off head is sandy-coloured, and a patch at the base of its wings is the same colour, giving the Buff-Tip its name. It looks for all the world like a broken birch twig, silvery on the outside bark with pale interior, even down to the pattern of wood grain. It has adopted that camouflage because birch is one of its caterpillar food plants, along with other native trees such as oak, hazel and alder.

Red Sword-grass is another master of disguise, and its scientific name, *Xylena vetusta*, means 'old wood'. When resting, its wings are wrapped tightly round its body, and with the mixture of rich red-brown and straw colour, it is brilliantly camouflaged. The working area of my garden, a place for cold frame and wheelbarrows, is covered in wood chip, and if I set a Red Sword-grass down among it, it instantly disappears.

If you look at an illustrated guide to moths, it can be confusing to begin with to see page after page of similar looking species. This is especially true of the Noctuids of which there are many brown moths that have just subtle differences, the LBJs or 'little brown jobs' that birders refer to. But it's these colours – beige, buff, tan, ochre or grey – that help them to blend in with leaf litter and tree bark.

A moth famous for its ability to imitate its background is the Peppered Moth, *Biston betularia*. Yet again, the species name shows the link to a plant, in this case betula or silver birch. It is often cited as an example of natural selection in action and referred to as 'Darwin's moth'. Peppered Moths are speckled black and white, and there are three forms in the UK: dark, light and intermediate. The colouring is like lichen on a tree trunk so the moth can hide in plain sight when resting in daytime. In the nineteenth century during the industrial revolution, when pollution from coal settled on trees and walls, the pale forms were much more likely to be predated on while the dark melanic form was more likely to survive and breed. Evolutionary change happened fast, and from the time of the first recording in Manchester of a black Peppered Moth, it took just forty-seven years for 98 per cent to be black.

With a reduction in air pollution in the mid-twentieth century, the result of the cleaner air was that lichen grew again on tree trunks that were no longer sooty. This time, it was the pale Peppered Moth that had the advantage and the dark that was more easily seen and eaten. It's now much more common to find the pale form, an amazing story that illustrates how this moth could respond to different environmental conditions.

Many moth patterns evoke those of lichen since it's a common background to rest upon. The Merveille du Jour is perhaps the most beautiful of all, and it always gives me a thrill when I find one in the autumn moth trap. This is a time when the ivy is flowering and the adults feed on this invaluable nectar source and on overripe berries. With its jade green, white and black markings, this moth could provide inspiration for fabric design. A female Merveille du Jour lays her eggs on oak branches or hidden in the cracks of the bark, one of the numerous insects hosted by oak trees.

Some species of moth disguise their wing shape using designs that break up their outline. Angle Shades, *Phlogophora meticulosa*, is one of these. Photographs help to pinpoint a moment in time, and I can still remember when I saw my first Angle Shades. A common day-flying moth, it was in the old walled garden where I worked, and I was completely blown away by its geometric patterns, the sculpted base of its wings like the scalloped edges of Gothic architecture. It was a revelation as I had no idea that moths could be so beautiful or that later I would go on to study them. The angles and shades that give the moth its name are a series of inward-pointing triangles, a visual trick that makes it look less like an insect and more like bits of dry leaf. Buff Arches, *Habrosyne pyritoides*, takes this even further and is a quite extraordinary creation. It's like a piece of psychedelic art where you don't know quite where anything is. Wings of smooth grey appear overlaid with orange markings in rounded zig-zags, all designed to confuse.

You wouldn't want to eat me

Camouflage is a clever way of protecting oneself. Another crafty technique is to pretend to be another insect altogether. The Hornet Moth, *Sesia apiformis*, has transparent wings with dark edges and a black and yellow body and, though it's harmless, it could be mistaken for a stinging insect. The upper wings of a Poplar Hawk-moth are a soft grey colour while the underwings protrude above them, giving this large insect a sculpted shape and a complexity that adds to its disguise. When disturbed and feeling threatened, this hawk-moth will repeatedly beat its hind wings to show a rufous patch that is normally hidden. The Eyed Hawk-moth, *Smerinthus ocellata*, takes this a step further, revealing a flash of bright blue, black-rimmed eyes as if a bird is looking at you.

Many caterpillars are hairy or have spines to deter predators. The Garden Tiger moth, *Arctia caja*, has a caterpillar that is known as a woolly bear, its dense coat of long ginger hairs a skin irritant. Several other species have irritant hairs for protection, so it's best not to handle them.

Tasting unpleasant, or pretending to, is another trick. Chinese Character, *Cilix glaucata,* is a moth that imitates a bird dropping! It has a resting position of wings folded upwards and with its rounded appearance – head and feet tucked away – and combination of creamy white, brown and grey, it's a perfect mimic. The curious name comes from some delicate silvery markings that suggested a character in the Chinese alphabet to those naming it, many of whom had a classical education.

Another name inspired by language is the Hebrew Character, *Orthosia gothica*, a commonly found species on the wing in spring and named after a clearly defined black wing marking. This is alternatively described as being like a Gothic arch (hence the specific name) or like the Nun character in the Hebrew alphabet (giving it its vernacular name). Many of these common names for moths were thought up by members of The Aurelian Society, Aurelian being an old word for lepidopterist. The society, which met in coffee houses and taverns, was one of the oldest zoological groups in the world, but in 1748, a fire broke out in the Swan Tavern, destroying their collections, records and library. Though the members escaped alive, they were so disheartened by the losses that they disbanded the group. Many of the fascinating names we have for moths come from their interests or observations. The Quakers, a group of moths with names such as Powdered, Common and Twin-spotted, were named after the muted clothes of the religious group. How I wish I could've been present to hear them discussing what names to invent and what flights of imagination led to Exile, Conformist and Shark.

Caterpillar disguise

Some of these fabulous names come from the shapes of caterpillars such as the grey chunky body of the Elephant Hawk-moth. The Lobster Moth, *Stauropus fagi*, a symphony of softest greys and browns, has a very different caterpillar; it looks like some strange scorpion or spider, all ridges and angles. If its appearance isn't enough to prevent it being eaten, it has a second defence. It will arch backwards, flailing its legs in the air, and squirt out formic acid. The Puss Moth, *Cerura vinula,* has a similar technique. When disturbed, it raises its head, displaying a red and yellow-rimmed face while waving twin tails, and can squirt formic acid at a potential attacker. It's a really striking caterpillar, its green body marked with a black, cream-edged saddle. Yet like the Lobster moth, the adult is much quieter with a furry cat-like appearance, undulating dark grey markings on silvery grey wings.

Many caterpillars disguise themselves as plant material. The Brimstone Moth, *Opisthographis luteolata*, looks like a knobbly twig, as does the Purple Thorn, *Selenia tetralunaria*. The Scalloped Hazel, *Odontopera bidentata*, is camouflaged to look like lichen and is one of the caterpillars known as loopers. It has no legs in the middle of its body so it moves along in a looping motion.

It's so much easier now to gain an insight into this secret world of eggs, caterpillars and well-disguised chrysalises thanks to modern technology. I always have my phone on me, ready to photograph wildlife in the garden, which is often just a fleeting moment. Close-up binoculars are a wonder, revealing the details of mosses, lichens, leaf veins, flowers and the many insects that live in these tiny landscapes. They can focus as near as a metre as well as being used for distance, so you can swap between birdwatching or checking on a far-off butterfly and then zeroing on its compound eyes or vibrantly coloured wings. My close-up binoculars are one of the best things I ever bought for wildlife watching. I can get lost in the miniature forests of moss, in the busy life of the soil, in the watchful eyes of a lizard – all these things happening in my garden that I couldn't see before.

4 How to Lure Moths and Butterflies

Grow the right plants

Butterflies and moths are so quick on the wing that they often pass by in a blur. It can be frustrating to try and photograph them as they move restlessly, feeding from flowers or jigging in flight to avoid predators. There are ways, though, of studying them by using a variety of types of lures. The first attraction is having nectar-filled plants in your garden that can draw butterflies and moths in from the surrounding area. Providing them with a range of species, each flower a different shape, makes the garden visually attractive to you as well as to butterflies. Often they will settle as they gorge themselves on the sweet liquid.

It helps to site plants out of the wind and to grow them at a height where you can easily watch insects as they feed. Buddleia is known as the butterfly bush for good reason, and it is heavily honey-scented. It's also very attractive to moths and if there's a flurry of grey wings, it is probably a Silver Y. Growing buddleia near a bench in a sheltered space will fragrance the air, and it makes a good cut flower, either fresh or dried; either way will scent the house. Despite the purple colour of the flowers, buddleias give a range of yellows when used for natural dyeing.

I've always grown buddleia in any garden that I've made, but conservationists often warn against planting it. This is because it produces a mass of seed and can be invasive, spreading readily onto adjacent land to the detriment of native plants. Buddleia was introduced from China in the late nineteenth century and it quickly naturalised, especially on waste ground or along railway lines where the currents of air can easily transport its tiny double-winged seeds. Seedlings can lodge themselves in gutters or cracks in masonry, causing damage.

I will still always grow it, though. To prevent seeding, I cut off the spent heads, which then allows the side shoots to develop, prolonging the flowering period. By the start of autumn, all the flowers have been taken off and the branches reduced to prevent wind damage over winter. Buddleias don't have a very big root ball and they can easily be yanked out of the ground by autumn gales. The following March, I will prune the branches back further, reducing the bush to a metre high. It grows quickly, and by the time it blooms, the flowers will be a good height for me to enjoy them. Left unpruned, they can be way above your head where you can't enjoy watching insects.

The new varieties of dwarf buddleias have so far not appeared to set seed, and they are suitable for small gardens, but there are many other plants for attracting butterflies: herbs such as marjoram, lavender, hyssop and thyme; native plants like red campion, primrose and clover; and ivy, which is a tremendous source of nectar in autumn. This is just a reminder that what we choose to grow in our gardens has a huge influence on what life we bring to them. There's a huge range of plants that you can grow to attract butterflies and moths, and my top choices are illustrated in the plant guide later on in this book.

It's fascinating to watch butterflies close up while they coil and uncoil their proboscis as they drink nectar. They are also attracted to overripe fruit, as you might see when they feast on fallen apples in an orchard. You can replicate this by putting out a dish of mushy bananas, and they will flock to its sticky sweetness; it's a great way for children to observe how they suck up their food. Alternatively, you can make a sugar feed, dissolving it in water heated in a saucepan at a ratio of one part sugar to ten parts of water. Once cooled, put it on a plate or use it to soak a colourful cloth or sponge and leave it among flowers.

Drunken butterflies

Butterflies are normally difficult to approach, flying off at the least movement, but you can get really close if they feed on fruit such as plums that are so overripe that they are fermenting. Sometimes they're attracted to tree sap. One time when I was walking in Culbin Forest on the coast near Inverness, I watched some fifty Red Admirals gorging themselves on the sap run that flowed down the trunk of a wounded tree. This is how early naturalists attracted moths so that they could study them. In 1842, Edward Doubleday, known as the Epping naturalist and with a particular interest in Lepidoptera, experimented with pasting a sticky mix of fermenting fruit and rum onto walls and trees. This became a popular way of luring moths, which could be checked by lantern light. Doubleday would go on to work at the British Museum, where he built up a comprehensive collection of butterflies.

As well as sugaring, as it is called, another method is making wine-ropes.

This involves soaking rags or absorbent cord in a mixture of sugar dissolved in red wine and hanging them from the low branches of a tree or a fence. Put out at dusk, it can be checked by torchlight (the red light on a head torch is best so it doesn't disturb the moths). This is a good way to attract the Old Lady moth, *Morma mauro*, a large-winged species of sombre colouring that reminded people of a mourning widow draped in a dark shawl. Its subtle markings are actually very beautiful.

Attracted to light

As new methods of lighting were invented in the nineteenth century, entomologists tried out various types of lamps, positioning them in front of a white surface such as a painted wall or a sheet. It was the invention of the Robinson trap in the 1930s that really transformed mothing. Lit by a 125w (or 160w) mercury vapour bulb, it produces beams of ultraviolet light that are visible to moths but not to humans. Having been attracted by its powerful bulb, the moths are funnelled down into a large container, essentially a huge black bucket where they can shelter from the glare in a collection of egg boxes. Because it's run by electricity, it needs to be near a power source. There are two other main types of moth trap, the Heath and the Skinner, and like the Robinson, they're all named after their inventors. Portable traps use a lithium battery or need a generator so they can be taken out into the field or used when on holiday. It's also possible to build your own.

There's quite a price difference in commercial traps, the Robinson being the most expensive. This is the kind that I use because it's the most effective and it's strongly built. It is important that raindrops don't touch the bulb since, although it's partially covered by a rain guard, it can crack. Because of the potential for mercury pollution if the bulb should shatter, these are being phased out, but there are still plenty available. It's a good idea to position a Robinson trap under an open-sided shelter if possible and, because I don't have a space like that, I don't set the trap in high winds or very rainy conditions. You should never look directly at a mercury vapour bulb as it can damage your eyesight and, as the light is very brilliant, it might be visible to neighbours. It also runs very hot and you should let it cool down before moving it. It does, though, produce the biggest catches of all the different systems.

Then there are actinic bulbs, which are cheaper to run. They produce light in blue wavelengths and they have quite a good catch rate. There are black light bulbs, which are less intrusive to the neighbours because they produce very little visible light as they emit ultraviolet and infra-red light. Some county moth groups have a loan scheme, and this is a very good way to begin an interest in these fascinating insects. Places with all-night lighting can yield good results and I know regular recorders who study the moths drawn to their porch light or, in the case of someone in my local Facebook group, an urban bus shelter.

Dark nights produce the best results because you're not competing with moonlight. Put the trap out shortly before dusk in a sheltered place: you can put a white sheet underneath it if you wish and consider the background. When moths settle outside the trap, it can be difficult to spot them among foliage; a plain wall is easier. Position it where it won't catch the early morning sun. Some dedicated mothers stay up half the night to check what species they are getting. I prefer to wait till morning! You do, though, need to be up before birds are active if possible because a robin or a wren can quickly learn that there's free food on offer.

It's a wonderful moment when you open a moth trap in the morning and discover what is inside. There's a feeling of expectation as each egg box is turned over. You need a notebook handy to jot down the species and a phone or camera to record any that are on the point of flying away. Lepidopterist suppliers sell a range of little plastic pots with lids and after a while, you get quite adept at containerising moths! One pot to each moth as otherwise they will bump into each other, causing damage. If you can't immediately identify them, you can put them in the fridge, which is especially useful if they are very flighty as the cold makes them settle still. A day in the fridge doesn't hurt them and they can be

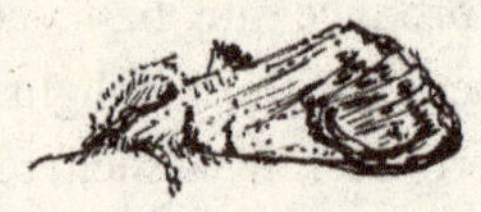

released in the evening. All moths are set free, either waiting till nighttime or by letting them go where they can be hidden by foliage. My favourite place for releasing moths is underneath the large leaves of some hostas.

There's a particular moment in the mothing year when the Large Yellow Underwings, *Noctua pronuba*, are at their height. They can be so plentiful in summer that the light trap is full of these vigorous, feisty moths. With their large size and heavy bodies, they crash into all the others, and the inside of the container can be covered in dust, the scales from their wings. It's a good idea to regularly wash out the bucket, and at LYU time of year (the common abbreviation for these pushy moths!), I wear a buff – a neckwarmer with which I can cover my nose – or a face mask so that I don't breathe in a lot of dust.

The Garden Moth Scheme requires setting a trap once a week between March and November so that everybody across the country is doing the same thing. This gives a framework for recording common moths in a standard fashion, leading to statistically robust data, and there are now well over 1 million records from all over the UK and Ireland. Mothing can become addictive, but it's advised not to trap every single night because this gives the insects no time to rest. I prefer once or twice a week to give them a chance to get on with their lives, to pollinate my plants and to breed future generations.

There's also a winter run of the Garden Moth Scheme for hardened enthusiasts and I did this one year, setting out the Robinson in the snow and ice! Living in a frost hollow in the north Pennines, I didn't think that I would be very successful, but I had a total of twenty-six moths in those three months, which was more than any of the others taking part in my regional group. I didn't repeat it, though, because it was quite an effort, and it feels good to have a bit of a break and come back to it fresh in the spring. As you build up data year on year, you become familiar with the different species and know what to expect. There's a comforting seasonality to the cycle, just as with yearly growth in the garden, and seeing the first Hebrew Character of spring, just as with the first Orange-tip butterfly, is like greeting an old friend. You can tell the time of the year as surely as seeing the first snowdrop or lifting the first potatoes.

Too much light

With moths being so sensitive to light, too much artificial light is disorientating for them and disturbs their natural behaviour. They use up energy that could instead be used for finding food or breeding; light pollution is a major disruption. They flutter around streetlights, confused and exhausted, and there's nowhere to hide, which makes them easy prey for bats. If you need outside lights, choose ones that point downwards rather than washing the sky with light, and turn them off when they're not in use. Research by Butterfly Conservation showed that moth caterpillar numbers in hedgerows under LED street lights were 52 per cent lower compared to those that were unlit, a massive over 50 per cent reduction in their reproduction. Light pollution impacts on many other forms of wildlife: blackbirds sing at nighttime, seasonal clues become confused, and fewer moths means fewer birds and mammals. Too much light even affects the growth of plants.

Moth trap interlopers

One of the fascinating side effects of setting a trap is the other insects that are drawn to the light. Opening the trap in the morning, I find a wonderful variety of wasps, midges, sexton beetles, lacewings and stone flies. It's a good clue as to what other wildlife you have in your garden, and there's even a Facebook group dedicated to these intruders. The sexton beetles are particularly amazing. Named after the sexton who would be in charge of the church graveyard, these are robust and chunky burying beetles that do an important job in the garden by recycling dead animals. They feed and breed on the corpses of mice, voles and small birds, and I've even watched them, over the period of some days, burying a dead hedgehog. Attracted by the smell, often from a very long distance away, males and females will meet up and mate at a corpse. They dig a hole beneath the dead animal so that it gradually settles into the ground and after burying it, the female lays her eggs on or next to the body. When the larvae emerge, both male and female care for them, which makes them very unusual in the insect world. As a side-effect of using light to attract moths, it's a great way of finding out what other life there is in your garden.

Irresistible lures

Some species of male moth are attracted from great distances by the pheromones given off by the female. You can buy synthetic lures to simulate this effect for clearwing moths and, for one of the most spectacular moths of all, the Emperor. This is a species that lives in wide open areas such as coastal dunes and heather moorland, and it's to the latter that I go in spring in the hope of spotting these incredible creatures. Female Emperor Moths, *Saturnia pavonia,* fly by night, settling into foliage, hidden and secret to us, a place where she can lay her eggs. Once there, she emits a powerful and irresistible scent from a gland at the tip of her furry abdomen to attract a male to mate. The Emperor has large antennae that are elaborately feathered to give an increased surface area for picking up her scent from up to three kilometres away.

A commercial chemical lure comes in a small vial or impregnated in a red rubber bung, sealed in a plastic bag, which you can store in the freezer for up to three years. I make my way up to the moors on a calm sunny day in May, the lure sealed in a small plastic container, and carrying a branch so that I can hang it at the right height. I unpack it carefully, making sure that I don't get the lure on my clothes or fingers. I had heard of a moth trapper who had accidentally touched the phial and then opened his car door. Result was he had several moths that wouldn't leave his car! Dropping the bung into the cut-off toe from a pair of tights, I hang this from the branch about three feet from the ground. I've barely put down my rucksack and straightened up before one arrives in a blur of orange and brown, a fast-paced, fluttering, gorgeous male Emperor Moth. His huge wings flap as he circles the top of the branch, and then two more males arrive, full of restless energy, bumping into my hair, twirling in the air, dancing around the lure. It's a thrilling experience.

These dramatically patterned moths fly between late March and early June, so that's the time to lure them before putting the sealed packet back in the freezer until the next year. They really are beautiful, the female being strikingly marked in silver and charcoal, with four large spots on her forewing that are as dark as owls' eyes. The male also has eye spots, but there's a flash of fiery burnt orange and umber from his underwings. He will zigzag low over the open ground searching for a female and when he scents her, will fly straight as an arrow towards the spot where she is hidden.

Artificial lures can also be bought for other species, and these make it possible to see clearwing moths, which are otherwise notoriously difficult to spot, although they fly by day. Their transparent wings are edged or marked with colour and are like stained-glass windows. Some are wasp mimics with yellow-and-black-striped bodies. There are fifteen species in the UK, many of which are considered scarce, but thanks to pheromone lures, they're becoming better studied and understood. They are most active in warm sunny weather in areas where their food plant can be found. Because it's been difficult to study them in the past, they are very under recorded, but more is now being learned about their distribution.

5
Gardening for Moths and Butterflies

Glowing in the dark

Sitting at dusk on my favourite bench in a sheltered corner of the garden, I watch the bowl-shaped flowers of evening primrose as they open up. Blooming by night as the name suggests, this is a plant that relies on night-flying moths for pollination. The pale, almost luminous colour is an advertisement, making for easier nighttime detection by insects. Mine is a favourite variety called *Oenothera stricta* 'Sulphurea', which doesn't grow taller than a metre and has reddish stems and leaves. Its unfurled buds are flushed in peach and they open to large, scented flowers.

I remember a story I was told years ago as I led a group from the Women's Institute around a garden. One member had grown up in a coastal Northumberland town and she described being able to see her way in the dark to the air raid shelter at the bottom of the garden thanks to the lines of evening primrose that grew along the path. It was such a perfect example of how pale or white flowers reflect moonlight as well as giving off scent to lure pollinators at the time when they are active.

It also illustrates how important I feel it is to make a garden that combines the needs of wildlife with how it looks. When they see my garden, so many people have an emotional response and comment on its beauty. They are moved by its flowing naturalism, colour and liveliness, and I think this is because it's ever-changing. To me, there is a joy in plants that sprout, grow, develop and seed that I don't find in varieties that stay the same for months on end. Many bedding plants are useless for insects, having been bred for larger flowers or double variants to the detriment of their reproductive parts. Petunias, begonias or busy Lizzies are frequently highly coloured and flower for ages but give nothing for pollinators. To me, they seem like plastic or dead plants. By making simple choices, we can achieve just as colourful a garden at the same time as it being active and alive.

Gardening for both wildlife and people is my overriding aesthetic. As gardeners, we can make a huge difference to nature. Adding up all the gardens in the UK has been estimated as totalling over 10 million acres, so we can make a real difference. We can grow wildflowers in our borders, allowing a bit of the countryside in, grow non-native plants that have nectar for adult insects, and mix and match as many varieties as possible at the same time as making it beautiful to look at. My garden has clearly defined path edges, an underlying form and structure that gives it a neatness and clarity that I find calming. The riotous informality is in the planting of the borders and the choices are ones that benefit insects. This is not rewilding because it is actively gardened rather than being left to do its own thing.

Astonishing biodiversity

An example of how sublime a garden can be, at the same time as being wildlife-rich, is the famous and historic Great Dixter in East Sussex. I love its atmosphere, full of self-sown plants, bees and butterflies, an experimental mix of the native and the exotic, and ever-changing throughout the year. Great Dixter is gardened with a soft touch, ox eye daisies frothing against paths and through borders, orchids flourishing in meadow grasses, Mexican daisies cascading down steps and among stones in the terraces. It is multi-layered in vegetation, not just in each border but also as it evolves through the year. It is these layers that mimic the wild and that have helped to make it so biodiverse. It is joyful, playful and packed with colour.

When a biodiversity audit was carried out at Great Dixter, everyone (ecologists especially) expected the wildlife value to be low compared to the countryside beyond. What it revealed, though, was surprising. Instead of the woodlands or meadows, the richest part of the whole estate was found to be the formal gardens. In just a handful of visits, the ecologists recorded over 2,300 species, including 130 species of bee, thirty-two species of butterfly, sixteen species of bumblebee, 220 species of spiders, including some national rarities, and over 400 species of moths. The lead ecologist said it was one of the richest sites he had surveyed and it changed the way he thought about gardens.

Great Dixter is a large and beautiful garden but it shows how complexity of planting leads to biodiversity. Even a small space can have very diverse habitats within it, and you can create these with a mixture of sun and shade, wet and dry soil, a variety of heights and a wide gamut of plant types. Small gardens, urban spaces, verges, rooftops: they can all add up to a significant contribution. By creating a long season of pollen- and nectar-rich plants, there is always something to supply the needs of insects, and they in turn feed many other creatures.

Perhaps the results at Great Dixter shouldn't have been so surprising because of the work of Jennifer Owen. Over thirty years from 1972, she made a study of her garden and recorded 2,673 species ranging from plants to mammals. She grew flowers and vegetables in a fairly ordinary-sized plot in suburban Leicester, where she made an inventory of the butterflies, moths, beetles, hoverflies and numerous other invertebrates as well as plants, mammals and birds. Jennifer avoided pesticides and grew a wide range of plants to form different height layers in the garden from trees, shrubs and perennials to ground cover. She was well ahead of her time in wildlife gardening.

We can learn from this. We don't need to re-wild to create a garden brimming with wildlife. It can be actively managed in a way so that it's good to look at and useful, providing vegetables for eating, cut flowers and visually pleasing borders. Layered planting, a long season of nectar- and pollen-giving plants, a combination of natives and non-natives, mixed habitats, bedding plants and varied flower structures all contribute to make a complex, dynamic garden ecology.

My own experience

So where to begin? My own garden was made from scratch fifteen years ago, so I know what it's like to start with bare ground. Though it was set around an old house, the land was in a similar state to many a new build, compacted from digger tracks and with rubbish buried under the soil. What we set about making was a mosaic of different habitats that also fitted in with the way that we wanted to live and enjoy being outdoors. A terrace front and back with places to sit. A vegetable garden for producing food. Compost heaps and working area. A greenhouse for seed sowing and a large ornamental flower garden that we could see from the house windows.

When we moved here, we found that the paving on the terraces had been very badly laid, but this was actually an advantage for my kind of gardening. The wide gaps between the stones provide microclimates into which plants can self-sow: Mexican daisies and white violas for hoverflies, verbena bonariensis and marjoram for butterflies along with French lavender and Corsican mint for scent. Wolf spiders live in the cracks and hunt across the paving, common lizards find safety between the stones, and there are numerous voles which, though not popular because they eat my plants, provide food for the tawny owls.

The compost heaps power the garden, providing lots of organic material, and the greenhouse is essential for living in a frost hollow. The lawn is really a green space, spongy with moss, a patchwork of grass, buttercup, daisy, clovers and speedwell, a foraging place for blackbirds. A rubble-filled corner became the right place to make a small meadow because of its lack of fertility, and it is now a picture with orchids, ox-eye daisies, yellow rattle, cowslips and ragged robin.

But it's the large flower garden, the most showy area, that is particularly rich in wildlife. Thanks to the trees that border the west boundary and provide leaf cover, there's a mix of soil types from damp to dry, and different light from sun-filled to shady. I planted it, thinking in terms of horizontal layers, to have many different niches and places for safety, food and shelter. Adding to the existing mature sycamores, I created descending heights from flowering shrubs, topiary for solid shapes, huge perennials high above my head, grasses, and alpines.

Moths and butterflies are an essential part of the whole ecosystem that my garden has become. Birds, spiders, amphibians and mammals, they all eat butterflies or their larvae. Night-flying moths are a food source for the bats that live here, of which we've recorded six species. Moths and their caterpillars are eaten by frogs, toads, lizards and slow worms, by spiders and other insects as well as by mammals such as hedgehogs. Winter Moths, *Operophtera brumata*, are a key food source for blue tits and great tits. Their breeding success is linked to the abundance of these pale green caterpillars, the ones that you see dangling on silken threads from trees. Blue tits time their broods to coincide with the emergence of Winter Moth larvae, and a single brood of blue tits can eat up to 10,000 caterpillars. I can watch the parent birds flying between their nest box and the sycamore trees, gathering beakfuls for their chicks. Sycamores are just one of a range of broadleaved trees and shrubs that these moths lay their eggs on; others include oak, beech and willow, and demonstrate just how important trees are in the cycle of the garden.

Very hungry caterpillars

It's also a good example of how we need to supply food plants for the larval stages of moths and butterflies. You can grow a wide range of flowering plants and these will attract butterflies and moths but, without food for their caterpillars, they won't be breeding and completing their life-cycle in your garden. I have a mix of native and non-native plants, flowers that come from all over the world and that we can grow in UK gardens. There are verbenas and dahlias from Mexico, rosemary and cotton lavender from the Mediterranean, peonies from China and echinaceas from America. Self-seeding through these are UK native plants such as sweet rocket, cow parsley, red campion and wild angelica. The wildflowers bring a soft informality to everything, threading among the borders, often bringing the joy of the unexpected or combinations that I wouldn't have thought of.

Sweet rocket, *Hesperis matronalis*, is found along the banks of rivers, often in different colour forms from purple through pink to white. I've limited mine to white because I like the way that the ethereal flowers seem to float above the borders. Like evening primrose, their petals glow in the dusk, which is the time when they give off a gorgeous spicy perfume. Sweet rocket is a member of the brassica (mustard) family, as are honesty, cuckooflower and hedge garlic. All are plants that attract Orange-tip butterflies, *Anthocharis cardamines,* such an uplifting spring sight. I grow hedge garlic, *Alliaria petiolata,* an edible wildflower with a tangy garlic taste, below the yew topiary – this is a plant you see along hedge bottoms and beside pavements. Cuckooflower, *Cardamine pratensis,* flourishes in gaps of the terrace paving. Both are said to be the favourite plants for Orange-tip butterflies to lay their eggs on, but it is on the sweet rocket I see a mass of emerging caterpillars, pale jade green with tiny black dots and black hairs. Their pupae (chrysalis) are camouflaged to look like thorns or seedpods and are attached with silk to a plant stem, the new butterflies emerging in spring. Orange-tip caterpillars eat the seed pods of the sweet rocket, so I make sure I grow plenty of plants so that they can still seed themselves.

A plant that sets abundant seed is mullein. There are a number of different verbascums from the slender *Verbascum phoeniceum* 'Violetta', which has dark-eyed purple blooms, but the one that towers over them all is the great mullein, *Verbascum thapsus.* It often grows on roadsides and waste ground, reaching up to two metres in height, striking and impressive with its huge yellow flower spike. Mullein leaves are covered in silver felt, and the wool gathered from their surface was once used in making candle wicks. Carder bees garner the fur from these leaves to build their nests, as they do with lamb's ears, *Stachys byzantina*. But it is the larvae of the night-flying Mullein moth, *Cucullia verbasci*, that create such a spectacular sight. Large chunky caterpillars, they are vividly patterned with bright yellow and black dots on white and as they feed, they leave a frass of round pellets. I don't mind that they can strip a plant of its leaves because they are so dramatic and beautiful to look at, fascinating to children and all part of the ecology of a living garden.

That's the thing with caterpillars, they feed on parts of plants – on leaves, seed pods, even roots – and we need to accept this as part of a flourishing wildlife garden. In the vegetable garden, cabbages and other plants can be protected by covering them, but in the flower garden, by growing a wide range in a naturalistic way, it's less noticeable if individual plants are eaten. Some moth caterpillars will only feed on a very limited range of species, sometimes even only one, so it's worth looking at a guide to caterpillar plants (see reading list at the back of this book) for the moths and wildflowers local to your area.

The value of trees

Trees and hedges are particularly valuable for insects. The young growth of blackthorn, *Prunus spinosa*, whose white flowers brighten hedges in spring and whose sloes are winter fruits for gin-making, is the food plant of the Brown Hairstreak butterfly, *Thecla betulae*. The oak, *Quercus robur*, not only a very beautiful tree but one that supports an astonishing 2,300 species of wildlife, hosts the caterpillars of the Purple Hairstreak butterfly, *Favonius quercus*, its species name denoting its link to the oak tree. And the lime-yellow Brimstone butterfly, *Gonepteryx rhamni*, its sculpted wings looking like newly emerged leaves, has larvae that feed on buckthorn, *Rhamnus cathartica*. Again, that food link is recorded in its specific name. When a Brimstone butterfly turned up in my garden, to my great excitement, it must have flown a very long way or got blown north on a south-west wind because its food plants don't grow in my area. If you're trying to identify a caterpillar, knowing what plant you found it on is a great help.

The bark of trees provides safe crevices into which some moth species can lay their eggs. The hardy Winter Moth, that important food source for blue tits, sees males on the wing during winter, but its females are flightless. They just have short stubby wings so they crawl up trees at dusk, giving off pheromones to lure males to them. If they are disturbed during mating, the male can carry the female to a safer place. Females then lay their eggs among cracks in the bark. These will hatch in spring into those dangling green caterpillars, timed to coincide with bud burst. They can 'balloon' on silk strands, using the breeze to transport them to a new food source.

The Vapourer, *Orgyia antiqua,* is another common moth species in which the female has only rudimentary wings though the male has orange brown wings with a pair of white eye spots and elaborately feathered antennae. Vapourers also live among broadleaved trees and shrubs, and can be found in parks and gardens. When the female emerges from her cocoon, she gives off pheromones to draw a male to her – hence those large comb-like antennae that can pick up her scent. She lays her eggs on top of the cocoon and when the caterpillars emerge in spring, they feed on a variety of trees such as blackthorn, oak, hazel and hawthorn. The hairy caterpillars are rather striking, coloured red and grey topped by creamy tufts like a line of Mohican haircuts. Some of our rarest moths – and most beautiful looking – depend on trees. I can only hope that one day I might see a Kentish Glory or a Broad-bordered Bee Hawk-moth. Moth and butterfly species vary throughout the country, some living in specific habitats, but I'm lucky to live near heather moorland with its glamorous Emperor moths.

Trees also host lichens, and these are a food source for certain moths such as the footmans. I get several different species to my light trap and I'm very fond of these graceful, neat moths. The Common Footman is warm grey in colour with apricot-coloured edges to the wings, which are curled gently over its body. When it rests, it looks a bit like a melon pip. The larvae eat lichen on trees, bushes, rocks and walls as well as hawthorn and bramble leaves. Lichens often provide a hiding place for insects that are camouflaged to their patterns such as the mottled umber moth or the amazing Merveille du Jour, *Griposia aprilina*, the well-named 'wonder of the day'. Elaborately marked in black, white and emerald-green, it is one of the most beautiful in the UK. Seen on a brick wall, it's visible; put it against lichen and it virtually disappears. And it's yet another insect whose larvae rely on oak trees.

If you're lucky to have oak growing in your area or in nearby city parks, these are some of the moths that you might attract to a light trap. But you can grow small trees in gardens such as silver birch, hawthorn, plum, acer or cherry. I have a pair of amelanchiers on either side of a bench, shrubs that are no taller than ten feet in height, and their branches are so draped with foliose lichens that in winter, they look as if they are covered in blossom. Many lichens depend on a lack of air pollution, but there are some that can tolerate it. What you can do is plant a mixed boundary hedge. This is a great general wildlife resource and its range of different species will also grow a variety of caterpillars. If you have the space, you can plant fruit trees and fruit bushes, and scramble honeysuckle, golden hop and ivy over fences, all of which will benefit birds, invertebrates and mammals as well.

Umbels and alliums

From trees and shrubs to perennials and alpines, the more variety and texture that you can put into a garden, the more it will attract wildlife. It will also make it more visually pleasing, full of colour, foliage and pattern. A couple of flower structures are particularly attractive to insects, and these are the umbels and the alliums. Think of cow parsley, dancing down road verges in long white clouds at the same time as the hawthorn is in flower, the essence of spring as in David Hockney's paintings. I grew up with the name Queen Anne's lace for this lovely wildflower, which better captures its airiness. Cow parsley is an umbel, a shape that has a mass of short flower stalks emanating from a central point like the ribs of an umbrella. The structure creates a cluster of closely set flowers so that insects don't have to travel far for food.

As I stand beneath a tall angelica, looking up at the flowers way above my head, I'm surrounded by a complete halo of flying insects. When angelica is at its peak, it gives us an astonishing amount of nectar and pollen, and the air around it is in constant movement from insect wings. This means that it produces a huge amount of seed, so I have to edit out plants that I don't want. From eight-foot-tall angelica down to the diminutive pignut, there's a multitude of umbels that bring a naturalistic feel to the garden. Some are annuals, really worth growing, such as the popular *Ammi majus* and *Ammi visnaga*, known as bishop's flower, a froth of white flowers, cloud-like and ethereal. The shorter *Orlaya grandiflora*, or white lace-flower, an annual that I grow in the borders as well as in pots, has ferny foliage and white flowers of special purity.

My garden is surrounded by sheep-grazed pasture, and there is a seed bank of wildflowers that germinates when the soil is disturbed. I think this is how I came to have pignut growing up through a carpet of flowering thyme on the way to the greenhouse. Delighted to give room to this tiny umbel with its finally cut foliage, I've let it seed into the thyme, and it now attracts sooty black Chimney Sweepers, *Odezia atrata*, day-flying moths whose caterpillars feed almost exclusively on its flowers and seeds.

There are many beautiful umbels to create a loose, wild effect. Baltic parsley, *Cenolophium denudatum*, a perennial that I grow at the front of my woodland border, is foamy and delicate. Scots lovage, *Ligusticum scoticum*, is a native plant with shining glossy leaves, red stems and white flowers opening from pink buds. And although I allow the wild cow parsley some free rein in the borders (deadheading many of the plants so it doesn't overdo it!), a more classy alternative is the purple leaved cultivar called 'Raven's wing'.

There are umbels too in the vegetable garden, and I let some of these go to seed: dill and fennel with their yellow-green flowers; coriander, which has decorative round spicy seedpods; celery, sweet Cicely and parsnip. A warning, though, about parsnip: it can cause a serious rash, a combination of exposure to sunlight with handling the plant, and other members of the umbellifer family can produce phytophotodermatitis. Allowing these vegetables to run to flower brings beneficial pollinating insects to the veg patch: flies, beetles, hoverflies, moths and butterflies, all part of a living, thriving garden ecosystem.

The other group of particularly valuable plants for insects is the allium family. These are some of the most decorative plants you can grow in your garden. They've become specially popular over the last years, starring in Chelsea gardens, used in formal and informal gardens alike. These ornamental onions with their rounded pom-pom flowers are nectar-rich for butterflies and moths, bees and hoverflies. In the vegetable garden, I cut some of the chives down in rotation so there's always plenty of fresh growth for cooking, but some are left to go to flower. Chives, garlic chives, leeks and Welsh onions, and the decorative forms of chives 'Pink Perfection' and 'Black Isle Blush' all add to the colourful mix. One year when I was visiting Swedish gardens, there was an influx of migratory Painted Ladies and the long rows of Welsh onions in the productive garden of Gunnebo Castle were covered in these beautiful butterflies. In my own garden, I have planted either side of the main path with *Allium christophii*, whose huge football-sized globes become alive with insects. Throughout the borders, I allow *Allium* 'Purple Sensation' to self-seed, its rounded flowers standing tall among the perennials.

Ivy and marjoram

To feed insects for as much of the year as possible, we need plants that flower outside the main summer explosion of plenty. Winter aconites open their cupped yellow petals when the temperature reaches 10°C, the same temperature that triggers buff-tailed bumblebee queens to emerge. Together with snowdrops, followed by other early spring bulbs such as crocuses, they have nectar in pollen starting as early as January, and mild days see the flowering of lungworts, excellent for bumblebees and dark-edged bee-flies. Lungworts are easy to grow, prettily patterned, and have pink to blue flowers that last for a long time. Perfect for ground cover in semi-shade, they can also be used to carpet the ground beneath later-emerging perennials.

The other end of the growing year sees a huge amount of choice with sedums, asters, dahlias and verbenas offering a smorgasbord for insects to feed upon before winter. One of the most important is the common ivy, which has two forms: the juvenile growth, which clings flat to walls and trees and, after about ten years, the adult growth when the leaves change shape and become less indented. Ivy then becomes more woody, its branches thickening, growing outwards and covered in flowers, then berries. This is when it's at its peak for wildlife, and an ivy-filled hedgerow on a late autumn day is thrumming with life. Bees, social wasps, moths, hoverflies, flies and late season butterflies such as Red Admirals cluster around its yellow flowers, often sunning themselves on the warm glossy leaves. Ivy's black berries are calorie-rich food for thrushes, blackbirds, redwings and blackcap among sixteen species of birds. Its network of branches make dense nesting places for birds and shelter for tawny owls. Its leaves are food for butterfly and moth caterpillars, such as Holly Blue butterfly and Swallow-tailed Moth. Ivy really is invaluable.

There are many top plants for butterflies and moths, and I've written about my favourites in the following guide, but ivy really is special, as is marjoram. When I first moved to this garden, I planted a herb border in the most sheltered spot between a grass path and a dry stone wall. It had some of the most free draining soil in the garden being close to the river and silty in nature. As some plants were lost in a winter of -18°C temperatures, hyssop, sages and curry plants succumbing to the cold and wet, it was the hardest marjorams that took over. It wasn't really what I intended and marjoram is a tremendous self-seeder but as with other accidental happenings in a garden, it's been a rather lovely result. A metre wide and ten metres long, the border is now purple from end to end, a glorious mass of marjoram flowers usually thronged with bees and butterflies. Until 2024.

That summer, I wrote in my *Country Diary* column for *The Guardian* about the shocking absence of insects on this bountiful resource. When the results of the Big Butterfly Count 2024 were published by Butterfly Conservation, they declared it a national 'butterfly emergency'. It was the worst summer in the Count's history. Possible reasons cited are weather extremes, climate breakdown, the use of pesticides and lack of habitat. This mustn't deter us from planting our gardens as richly as possible for insects; in fact, it's the one thing that we can do across the whole of the UK, as well as calling on councils and public bodies to play their part. Nature has an amazing way of bouncing back. Just look at the incredible results achieved in a short space of time by the Knepp Castle Estate in West Sussex, which now has the largest population of Purple Emperor butterflies in the country among many of the rarities: turtle doves, nightingales, nightjars and raptors. If anything, it makes me more determined to make my garden as hospitable as possible for all forms of life, to offer up plentiful food, shelter, water and nest sites, and do what I can in my small way. The annual RSPB Big Garden Birdwatch and the Big Butterfly Count become even more valuable in demonstrating the state of wildlife in the country. Without these, it would just be anecdotal and there wouldn't be evidence of what is happening. Trapping moths on a regular basis, collecting data to help build up a picture, is my way of helping.

Long grass, nettles and sheds

Many of the moths that are attracted to my light trap are micro-moths. Some, such as the prettily patterned Mother of Pearl, *Patania ruralis*, and the Small Magpie, *Anania hortulata*, are actually bigger than some of the macro-moths! The sizing seems a bit arbitrary. Many are very small, often overlooked, but an important part of a wildlife garden, food for many birds and other forms of life. There are species that fly in daylight, the kind that you disturb when you walk through grasslands that quickly disappear again when they line up with a grass stem. There are over 1,600 species of micro-moths in the UK and identification can be tricky. It's another good reason for having longer grasses in your garden or a small meadow, as well as making a corridor for mammals, slow worms and amphibians. My mini meadow is added to by one-metre-wide fringes of long grass around the lawn, and this is not only a habitat for micro-moths but also for butterflies. Meadow Brown and Ringlet, Speckled Wood and Gatekeeper, skippers and Marbled White, these are all butterflies that are attracted to grasslands.

Over the back wall of my garden, on a slope that leads down to the river, is a wild area of nettles, docks and ground elder. Much as the compost heap powers the vegetable garden, this holds the key to the abundance of many of the garden butterflies. Nettles are well known as food plants for the caterpillars of Comma, Small Tortoiseshell, Peacock and Red Admiral, and if you can leave a patch where they won't be a problem for the garden, it is a great help. Because they're separated from the veg garden by the stone wall, they don't seed or creep into the cultivated area. The area where the nettles grow is in the sun, which butterflies prefer when they're looking for places to lay their eggs. Moths also breed among nettles, common species such as Mother of Pearl, Burnished Brass, Beautiful Golden Y and Snout. And many other invertebrates have been recorded on these much maligned plants.

It's fascinating to look for caterpillars among nettles. They are unaffected by the stinging hairs of nettles, so this gives them protection from predators. The larvae of both Small Tortoiseshell and Comma butterflies roll the leaves around themselves as they are feeding. Small Tortoiseshells can be seen in communal groups, protecting themselves with a silk webbing tent that they build around nettle tops, emerging to bask or to feed. The botanical name for nettles being *Urtica*, this is reflected in this butterfly's scientific name of *Aglais urticae.* Once the spiny, black and yellow caterpillars have devoured a nettle top, they move onto the next, leaving the webbing behind as they grow, which is full of shed skins. If threatened, they move in a synchronised twitch like a Mexican wave to confuse a predator. When ready to pupate, they crawl away separately. Although they are suffering a worrying decline, Small Tortoiseshells are found throughout the UK, even in Orkney and Shetland.

Perhaps this is because nettles are so ubiquitous, found anywhere where the soil is nitrogen-rich, such as waste ground and places disturbed by agriculture.

Comma butterfly caterpillars used to frequent the hop fields of Kent, the garden of England, along with the Pale Tussock moth, which was known as the hop dog. Londoners would leave the East End *en masse*, catered for by special trains, for the annual hop harvest. Whole families, from grandparents to babies, would decamp for the hop holiday to earn money and to escape the city. With the reduction in hop fields, Commas went into sharp decline but have recently bounced back, even to the extent of moving north. When I first moved to Northumberland it was rare to see a Comma, but now they often visit my garden, thanks to those nettles in the wild area over the wall and the golden hop that grows over a homemade willow arch in the vegetable garden.

A sanctuary of a different sort, a man-made structure that can hold surprises, is the garden shed. Most butterflies and moths spend the cold months in their larval stage, generally as pupae, sometimes as eggs. But how many of us have found overwintering butterflies tucked into spaces around house windows or in dark corners? British winters are too cold for adult butterflies to stay active and they seek shelter in quiet, cool places where they remain in a dormant state similar to hibernation. Once the heating comes on, or if sunlight pours through a window warming a room, they may wake up. Then you can relocate them somewhere cooler such as a shed or garage. The butterflies most likely to roost over winter are Small Tortoiseshell and Red Admiral, Comma and Peacock, and they often make their way into sheds. These are a more suitable temperature than houses. Alongside butterflies, you might find a beautiful moth called The Herald, *Scoliopteryx libatrix,* which before we built houses would have found shelter in caves. With its scalloped edge and colouring of bronze and orange, it is really handsome, camouflaged to look like autumn leaves.

Evening scents

Brushing against lavender on a warm summer's afternoon, squeezing a sprig of lemon verbena, cutting dill and coriander for cooking: these are all uplifting moments in the garden. Fragrance is an essential part of my garden, adding another sense to the whole experience. Flower scents are used by plants to seduce pollinators and though they're not designed just for our benefit, we can enjoy them! Night-scented flowers are reaching out to lure moths, and by planting them we're not only attracting these wonderful and varied insects but creating an evening garden that cries out to be enjoyed. A city courtyard with its sheltering walls will hold in the evening air. A bench surrounded by evening-scented plants becomes a place to relax deeply.

Some of these are climbers with which to cover walls and fences, a useful disguise that makes a garden feel larger by greening the boundary as well as holding nest sites for birds. Honeysuckle has long tubular flowers that can only be accessed by insects with long tongues. Jasmine carries an exotic scent of the Mediterranean. Others are the evening primrose that I grow around my bench, night-scented stock, a small pink flowered annual that exudes a powerful perfume, and the tobacco plant, *Nicotiana alata,* which can be grown in pots or in flower beds. The taller species, the beautiful white *Nicotiana sylvestris*, has clusters of very long tubular flowers. Native British moths can't reach its nectar, but it is accessible to the immigrant Convolvulus Hawk-moth, which, like the other hawk-moths, is a spectacular insect.

Pleasing scents are well known to have a positive effect on our well-being. They're very personal, and can trigger memories. When I smell the sweet orange blossom of philadelphus, I'm immediately taken back to a garden in Spain. The tanginess of nasturtium leaves, the spiciness of pinks, the pungency of rosemary, these all take me straight back to my childhood. Scented gardens are valuable to those with dementia or with sight loss, and there are plants that can give scent all year round. As their function is to attract pollinators, this has the dual effect of providing food for insects.

Winter scent is especially valuable. Just knowing that it's there becomes a reason to go outside, even when there's little else in flower. Daphnes are shrubs with intensely fragrant winter blooms, compact enough for small gardens. Planted in a warm sheltered position near a wall or by door, the smell doesn't get blown away by the wind. They offer a source of nectar for bees and other insects at a time when many other plants haven't yet emerged. Many winter flowering shrubs have small flowers but they exude heady scents to attract the few pollinators that are out. There's sweet box, *Sarcócocca*, with small creamy white flowers among glossy evergreen foliage; winter honeysuckle, a bushy shrub with creamy white tubular flowers; and *Viburnum farreri*, pink-flowered and spicy. Wintersweet with small white flowers on bare branches, and *Mahonia* 'Charity' holding long sprays of pineapple-scented yellow flowers. Witch hazel, or Hamamalis, is a very lovely shrub with orange-red autumn foliage, but it's in late winter that it entices you out into the garden with its colour and sweet, spicy scent. The flowers are curious looking: yellow, orange or red with narrow petals that are often described as spidery. Its branches grow in defined Y shapes and they've been used as dousing rods for underground water. I've planted mine in front of some yew topiary and in line with the house windows so that I can see its flowers lit up against the dark green background. Nectar so early in the year is valuable to many insects, and witch hazel is fed on by butterflies, bees and moths including Satellite, *Eupsilia transversa*. This fairly common moth has white or orange markings – a round planet-like circle with two small satellites either side. It's a moth that you can find on mild days throughout winter and is one that can't be mistaken for anything else.

The scent of phlox is another of my childhood plants: evocative, sweet and floral, it conjures up full flowing cottage gardens. The flowers of the tall border-type of Phlox have long corollas and the nectar can only be accessed by long-tongued insects such as butterflies, moths and certain bumblebees. Phlox come in a range of colours from scintillating red through brilliant purple to whites and pinks. It's these pale colours that are visible in evening light, glowing at dusk, and giving off perfume to advertise itself to pollinators. And although it's called night-scented phlox, *Zaluzianskya ovata*, it is in a different botanical family, equally heavily scented, flowering from June to September and a good food source for moths. If you haven't the space for border phlox, this is a neat and low growing alternative, a white-flowered alpine for containers or raised beds.

The result, a garden full of life

It's an evening in August and the late light comes flaring through the petals of orange poppies and blue cornflowers. It's a magical transformation that so often happens here as the sun is setting on my garden, and one of the things that makes me love it so much. I write in my diary:

> *Then the light came, as usual about 7.30, suffusing the whole garden with brilliancy, turning all colours into that extra dimension that is normally hidden. Every hair shines along the stems of red campion, penstemons glow ruby, lilies trumpet joyfully, and the stone walls are touched with gold.*

The fields to the west are long with grass, thistle down glows as it floats, gnats dance up and down, and the swallows are flying in great looping circles, feeding on tiny grass moths before their great migration south, chattering as they fly. And as the light dips, the patterns they describe in the sky give way to the similar sweeping flight of bats. All this life, the whole experience that the garden is and the many things that live here are dependent on the insects that are only here because of the way it is planted. The great wealth of plants of many different shapes and colours, the multilayered flower beds, the complexity and freedom of the interwoven borders, all add up to a garden that is full of life.

6
Illustrated Guide to Host Plants for Moths and Butterflies

Moths and butterflies rely on nectar and pollen for food, so the best way to help them and to attract a wide range of species is to provide for them all year round. When I ran the specialist nursery at Chesters Walled Garden, I got involved with planting up gardens for pollinators at local schools. One year, Northumberland National Park had a programme in which school children were each given six plants that they would take home and plant in their own gardens. The idea was to inspire the children but also that they would talk to their parents about why these particular plants were chosen. The six were to give a selection throughout the year, and I remember cowslip and bugle being among them. It was on a small scale with just a few chosen plants but the basic idea is there: to provide for insects in as many seasons as possible.

The spring period of March to May sees a profusion of flowering bulbs in gardens such as crocus, grape hyacinth, hyacinth, scilla and chinodoxa. Hellebores and lungworts flourish in semi-shaded borders with moist soil and good leaf mould. Bugle spreads into carpets of ground cover, with its spires of blue flowers. Out in the open where it is sunny, early flowering heathers are excellent forage for bees, and native cowslips and primroses (not the highly bred polyanthus of garden centres) will seed themselves.

There's plentiful food in the summer garden but some of the best are alliums, perennial cornflowers, hardy geraniums, scabious, catmint, chives and ornamental thistles. Verbenas start flowering in summer and go well on into autumn, providing a really long season as well as looking beautiful. From August into October, they are joined by Michaelmas daisies, sedums, cardoons, coneflowers, Joe Pye weed, sea hollies and the open type of dahlia, adding up to a colourful fanfare of a finale. And, as I said before, one of the best things you can grow to give energy to insects as they head into winter is common ivy.

The following is my choice of just some of the many plants that you can grow to benefit moths and butterflies. Some are poisonous, so please check before planting as I generally haven't mentioned whether they are toxic or not. A lot of my choices are because they are the food plants for caterpillars, and are often less considered than the well-known flowers that are recommended for pollinator gardens. I've already described some of the top plants – for example, evening primrose and ivy – and I'm concentrating in this guide on garden plants, wildflowers and hedging material.

Moth caterpillars may eat specific parts of a plant. Some eat the buds or flowers, or the seeds and fruit, the roots, leaves, dead leaves, or may even feed inside the stem. If you want to learn more, there's a list of books at the back in the bibliography. Some moth larvae are polyphagous, meaning that they can eat many different types of food. Others need just one food source, and this is where we gardeners can really help. It's a fascinating subject.

Bird's foot trefoil, *Lotus corniculatus*

This vibrant native plant makes spreading pools of gold alongside roads, in open ground and in rocky places where there is sun and good drainage. It's a long-lived, low-growing perennial, its pea-like flowers changing from bright yellow to orange-red as they age. Because of these dual colours, it is also known as eggs and bacon, and it flowers continuously from May to September.

I grow bird's foot trefoil in a navy blue ceramic pot, the contrast between the complementary colours making it really stand out. It also means that I can easily deadhead it and, as lots of seed is produced, this is a way of reducing its spread. It's also in my little meadow where it can just do its own thing. If you do allow it to seed, the pods are black and curving with a sharp point, and that inspired its name of bird's foot and many colourful alternative names such as devil's toenails and hen and chickens.

Bird's foot trefoil, like other legumes, is a nitrogen fixing plant as well as making nutritious grazing in hay and silage. It's a good source of nectar for many insects including wasps, bees and bumblebees. But it is especially valuable for being the larval food plant for a number of moth and butterfly species: for the Common Blue, Green Hairstreak and Dingy Skipper butterflies as well as the Six-spot Burnet moth. Common Blue larvae have a fascinating interaction with ants that tend them in return for sugary substances.

Catmint, *Nepeta* 'Six Hills Giant'

There's a number of different catmints that are great for insects, but this is my favourite because it so free-flowering, large and showy. I grow it either side of a central path, intersecting with the sedum path, so that both are a smorgasbord for insects. As the name suggests, this is a particularly giant

catmint and it needs to be grown back from the edge so that when it flops, which it does attractively, it softens the path but doesn't completely swamp it.

Big and bushy, 'Six Hills Giant' was named after a Hertfordshire garden about 100 years ago so it's been in cultivation for a long time. It has aromatic, silvery leaves, and cats sometimes are drawn to it, though it's not as magnetic to them as catnip, which is *Nepeta cataria*, whose dried leaves are used in cat toys. An incredibly adaptable plant, you can grow it almost anywhere, and it makes a good alternative to lavender if you can't grow that. After its first flush, catmint can be cut back for a second wave or left to sprawl and soften in colour.

Bumblebees and butterflies are drawn to its flowers as well as Silver Y moths, an agitated blur of wings. It's a caterpillar food plant for the little Mint moth, *Pyrausta aurata*, which flies by both night and day and is a little gem with a golden yellow spot. It feeds on various herbs in the mint family, including marjoram, thyme, catnip and clary sage.

Clover, *Trifolium* spp

Threaded throughout the green space that is my lawn are various types of clover, their flowers white, yellow or, where the grass is longer, red. Bumblebees forage in the flowers, which have abundant nectar, and there are also solitary bees. Red clover, *Trifolium pratense*, can fill out more in my mini meadows and it's the caterpillar food plant for several moths. White clover tends to dominate in lawns because of mowing. Luckily, many gardeners no longer see this as a problem that needs controlling with selective weedkillers but instead enjoy the spangling of white flowers.

Some moths, such as Hebrew character, Silver Y and Six-spot Burnet, are generalists, feeding on a variety of different clovers.. Clouded yellow butterflies, *Colias croceus*, migratory species from southern Europe and North Africa that regularly visit Britain, feed on red or white clover and, with the abundance of clover in farmland, can breed. When they arrive *en masse*, these times are known as clouded yellow years. Their other food plant is bird's foot trefoil. Beautiful butterflies, they are bright yellowy-orange, a much warmer colour than Brimstone, while their closed wings look yellowy green.

Other clovers to grow are *Trifolium rubens*, the ruddy clover, which has soft silvery tops that open into feather-like ruby-red flowers. A perennial, it stays in a neat clump, self-seeding in a minimal way. Crimson clover, *Trifolium incarnatum*, is a green manure plant with deep red flowers used for smothering weeds in the vegetable garden and fixing nitrogen.

Echinacea, *Echinacea purpurea*

Daisy flowers are among the very best at attracting insects because of their open generous structure. Echinacea, also known as coneflower, is like a child's simplified drawing, with petals radiating from a central cone. It has bold purple flowers and has become popular recently for its perfect pairing with ornamental grasses in prairie-like planting schemes. This is a flower that needs full sun and well-drained soil, but even then it's often not very long-lasting as a perennial. Seed grown from the species tends to fare a bit better.

There are now lots of colours of echinacea on offer, from the purity of 'White Swan' through apricots, multicoloured, reds and oranges to the unusual 'Green Jewel'. Leave the seed heads on all winter for the striking central cones, only cutting back when you start to see new growth emerging. They don't like being disturbed so once planted should be left alone, and they look wonderful in large drifts.

Butterflies such as Painted Lady, Red Admiral, Small Tortoiseshell and Peacock can land on that central cone, working their way round, probing each individual disc floret. It's this flower structure that makes daisies so easy for insects to feed from, and it's on similar plants that I notice so many butterflies: the yellow *Inula hookeri*, with its furry buds and fine rayed daisies; the richly toned heleniums, with their red, orange or yellow flowers; and the vivid annuals, marigolds and zinnias, that we grow in the veg garden.

Foxglove, *Digitalis purpurea*

A quintessential cottage garden plant, the foxglove is a British native that looks equally good in a contemporary scheme. A biennial, it grows fast from a basal rosette of leaves to tower over other border plants. Bumblebees reach up into its magenta tubes using their long tongues to feed from the nectar. The flowers have spotted throats as a guide for bees and are arranged to one side of the stem, opening in sequence from the bottom up. Occasionally, they can have a mutant flower at the top, one huge open bell, an abnormal fusion of flowers known as a terminal peloria.

Foxgloves produce great quantities of seed, and you can collect this so that you can distribute it exactly where you want new plants to grow. The best way is to line a wheelbarrow with a large sheet of newspaper, sprinkle the dry seed in and use the crease in the paper to funnel the contents into a paper bag. The seeds need light to germinate, which is why so many grow after a woodland is felled. As well as the usual purple, white foxgloves occur both in the wild and in the garden, and sometimes people stick to just the whites for their borders.

Important cardiac drugs are derived from foxgloves, and all parts of the plant are highly toxic. The Foxglove Pug, *Eupithecia pulchellata*, is another example of a moth named after its caterpillar food plant, but the leaves are also host to both Large and Lesser Yellow Underwing, Small Angle Shades, Purple Clay and the delightful Frosted Orange.

Fuchsia

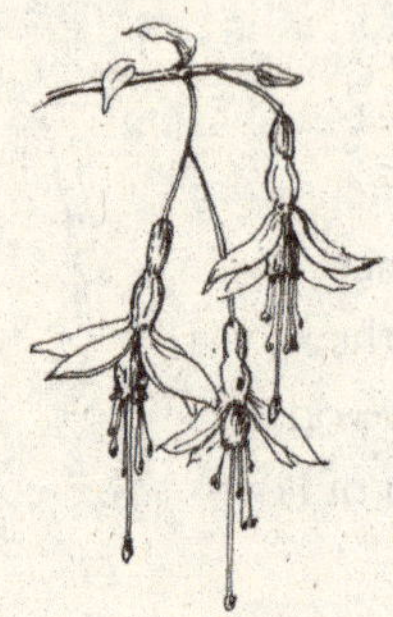

Garden centres in spring are packed full of the enticing colours of bedding plants, often impulse buys chosen for their visual impact. What may be less thought about is whether or not they have any wildlife value. Of the usual bedders, tuberous begonias bloom non-stop and have intense bright colours, but with their big hybridised flowers, they have almost zero nectar. Another choice, and an equally popular bedding plant, is the fuchsia. Although this comes from South America, the leaves are eaten by the caterpillars of some of the most fabulous hawk-moths: Elephant, Bedstraw, Striped and Silver-striped Hawk-moths, and perhaps this is because they are in the same family as the willowherbs. The caterpillars themselves are so striking that it's a joy to find them.

On the West Coast and Ireland, it's common to see fuchsia hedges, which in some cases are even out-competing native hedging plants. These are *Fuchsia magellanica*, which is hardier than bedding plants and can be easily clipped to shape. In inland areas that are more prone to frost, it can be grown as a bush and cut to the base every year like a perennial plant. The flowers are graceful red droplets like earrings and are very attractive to bees. As a species plant, they are more delicate in form than the larger cultivars. But it's these more blowsy flowers that are very suitable for growing in containers, and you could be rewarded by the sight of one of the spectacular hawk-moths.

Golden hop, *Humulus lupulus* 'Aureus'

If you want to disguise a shed or cover an arbour, this energetic climber has vividly lime-green leaves that look wonderfully fresh in spring. It will scramble up and cloak a fence to blur your boundary, making a garden appear larger than it is. In late summer, the greenish-yellow aromatic flower clusters are draped in swags and by autumn, the leaves turn golden. Male and female flowers grow on separate plants so you need female hops for flowering. The hops can be used as dried flowers, great tresses of them making garlands, and the pressed leaves for making art.

It's easy to propagate golden hop since it spreads out underground, sending out runners that can be separated from the main plant. That does mean that it can be a bit overenthusiastic, creeping out into a border, though I don't find it too difficult to control. It needs a strong arch or support for the weight and to stand up to wind. The leaves fall in autumn and I then use the vines to twist into decorative wreaths. Cut it to ground level over winter and it will quickly climb back up again in spring. The hairy leaves can be a skin irritant so wear gloves when handling them, and hops are toxic to cats and dogs.

Look carefully among its leaves and you might see the caterpillars of Comma butterflies or of several types of moth: Currant Pug, *Eupithecia assimilata;* Buff Ermine, *Spilosoma lutea;* Pale Tussock, *Calliteara pudibunda*; or Buttoned Snout, *Hypena rostralis.*

Grasses

It doesn't take much space in a garden to incorporate a small perennial meadow. I started with an area no larger than a few paces wide, which I then extended into metre-wide strips around the lawn. Invaluable for wildlife, it's a place for slow worms, frogs and toads, small mammals, fungi and insects. It is cut in late summer and everything raked off to keep the fertility low, but some parts such as the base of the stone walls are left undisturbed for hibernating caterpillars or chrysalises. Wildflowers are sprinkled throughout but grasses are also very important.

Native grasses are wind pollinated, so they don't produce nectar, but they are the food plant for a number of British caterpillars. In my garden, I see Small Skipper, Ringlet, Speckled Wood and Meadow Brown butterflies, but grasses are needed for many others such as Scotch Argus, Wall, Mountain Ringlet and Gatekeeper. Some species scatter the eggs while flying. Ringlet will choose to fly above fescues and cock's foot grasses while Gatekeeper is less selective.

The list of moths whose larvae feed on grasses is really extensive. Each has a different specialism: for example, Slender Brindle needs quaking grasses and wood melick, Grass Eggar feeds on the marram grass that stabilises sand dunes, and Ear Moth on saltmarsh grasses. Fine grasses are best for garden meadows as they are less vigorous, so if you grow fescues you might attract Map-winged Swift, Lunar Yellow Underwing and the delightful little Antler moth.

Hawthorn, *Crataegus monogyna* and Blackthorn, *Prunus spinosa*

Along with making a pond, planting a mixed native hedge is one of the best things that we can do for wildlife in our gardens. Hedges filter the wind, standing up to gales much better than fences. They provide nest sites and food for birds, flowers for insects, food plants for caterpillars, nuts and fruits for squirrels and small mammals, and are green and restful on the eye.

Two of the trees that are often included in mixed hedges are hawthorn and blackthorn. Both have white flowers, blackthorn flowering early before its leaves grow, and that period in early spring when the weather can be fierce is known as blackthorn winter. The bushes are crowded in star-shaped white flowers, food for bees and hairstreak butterflies, and you know that there will be autumn fruits to look forward to, sloes for making delicious gin. The only thing to watch out for is the vicious spines, which can cause serious infections.

Hawthorns also have spines capable of causing infection so I always wear thick gloves when pruning them. Also known as the May tree after the month when it is out, the time of hawthorn's flowering, which coincides with verges frothing with cow parsley, is one of the magic moments of spring. There is an extensive list of moths and butterflies that lay their eggs on blackthorn and hawthorn, many common species, some rarities, and too many to mention, but it shows how vital it is to choose plants carefully when making a new hedge.

Heathers, *Calluna* and *Erica* spp

When I first started gardening professionally, heathers and conifers were all the rage, grown for their apparent low maintenance and year-round interest. Even then, I found them boring because they didn't

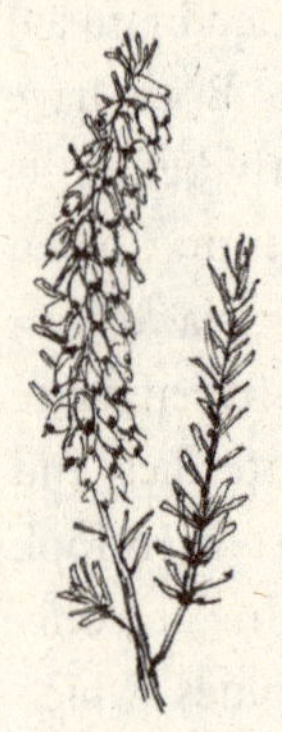

move and I felt I related more to planting that evolved throughout the year, developing and changing with the seasons. Having fallen out of fashion for years, they are now being reassessed and incorporated into contemporary designs that are not so one-sided. Notice what bees are attracted to winter-flowering heathers and it's obvious how much nectar they produce at this lean time of year.

Naming is not always a clue. The Small Heath butterfly, *Coenonympha pamphilus*, small and quietly coloured in pale orange, is found on heathland, but its caterpillars feed on find grasses such as fescues, whereas larvae of the Common Heath moth, *Ematurga atomaria*, do feed on heather. The males of the rare Silver-studded Blue butterfly, *Plebejus argus*, flash silvery blue wings as they fly low over the heath.

Some species of heathland plants need acidic soil, but varieties of *Erica carnea* are more adaptable. Several species of bumblebee as well as honeybees feed from heather flowers, as do also hoverflies and solitary bees. There are numerous species of moth whose caterpillars feed on heather, just some being Fox Moth, eggars, Magpie, Early Thorn, Ruby Tiger and of course the glamorous Emperor Moth that responds to a lure. In the garden, we might find True Lover's Knot, a romantically named moth with red and brown Celtic knot patterns.

Honeysuckle, *Lonicera periclymenum*

This is a perfect example of a garden plant that gives pleasure to us as well as having great value for wildlife. Honeysuckle will scent the air of an evening, its fragrance being sweet or spicy depending on the variety, and there are many to choose from. If you can grow it in a sheltered place, such as a town yard, the scent will be held within the walls. Our native honeysuckle grows in woodlands and in hedges, its roots having a cool, moist run in leaf mould-rich soil, its twining stems clambering up through trees to reach the light.

Wild honeysuckle has clusters of white and pink flowers, their deep tubes only accessible to insects with long tongues such as moths. To attract them, it has evolved to give off its scent by night. You can grow honeysuckle over a fence, use it to disguise a shed or let it climb up through roses. The flowers are followed by bright red berries (poisonous to us but good for the birds), and there are other species or cultivars with cream, orange or raspberry-red flowers.

A great variety of moths feed from the flowers, or their caterpillars eat the leaves. This includes some of the most beautiful: Scalloped Oak, Copper Underwing, Leopard Moth and the aptly named Beautiful Golden Y. Adult Elephant Hawk-moths can detect honeysuckle from a long way off, and growing this important native plant is a great way to attract moths to your garden.

Lady's smock, *Cardamine pratensis*

This dainty little wildflower is related to other food plants of Green-veined White and Orange-tip butterflies. Also known as cuckoo flower, it has a charming simplicity with four small pale pink or mauve petals with delicate mauve veining arranged in the cruciform shape of the brassica family. This shows its relationship to garlic mustard, honesty and sweet rocket, all plants that these two butterflies lay their eggs on.

Lady's smock grows in damp places such as the sides of streams, meadows and ditches, so it's best to find a moist area of the garden to grow it in. I have planted it into my small meadow but it has now migrated, its seeds finding their own niche in the spaces in between the terrace stones. Here, it is thriving, even though the paving is baking hot in summer, probably because of the cool soil tucked down below the gaps. Voles and mice like to nibble the leaves, which have a hot mustard taste.

From my bench on the terrace, I can watch Orange-tip butterflies, the males with their bold orange markings, the females more subtle, fluttering above the plants of lady's smock. This is such an uplifting sign of spring and I get such a buzz when I see the first Orange-tip butterfly of the year. Later, I might spot the tiny orange eggs, just one laid on each plant because of the cannibalistic nature of the green caterpillars, which hatch around the end of June, feeding up until they can form a chrysalis for overwintering.

Lavender, *Lavandula* cultivars

The flowers of many of our favourite garden herbs are very attractive to adult stages of insects. Many of these plants come from the Mediterranean so they're not so useful for native caterpillars, but their wealth of nectar means that they are buzzing with bees and busy with butterflies. Sage, marjoram, hyssop, thyme, savory and catmint: all are highly scented, beautiful to look at, and an essential part of any garden.

Lavender has been grown for centuries, valued for its purple flowers and its scent used in household products and for cooking. It was a staple of the still room in a medieval household, a place where recipes were made for perfumes, room fragrances, ointments and furniture polish. Freshly washed linens were laid on lavender hedges for the scent; the word lavender comes from the Latin *lavare*, which means to wash.

To make the most of lavender, plant it where you will encounter it frequently such as either side of a path to the front door or surrounding a seating area. It needs full sun and well-drained soil, pruning back after flowering to keep it compact or in early spring in colder areas. Butterflies that come to its nectar include Comma, Small Tortoiseshell, Painted Lady, Red Admiral and Common Blue. A flurry of wings in the daytime might be a Silver Y moth or a Hummingbird Hawk-moth, both immigrants that are more plentiful in some years than others, making their way north on southerly breezes.

Marjoram, *Origanum vulgare*

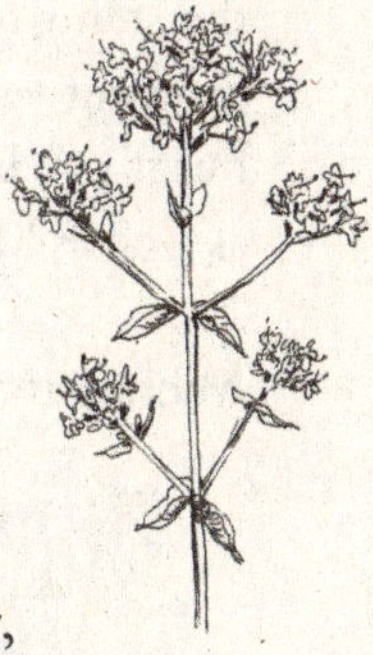

When I made my current garden, I planted herbs in a long border running alongside the vegetable garden. Gradually, because I didn't keep a close enough eye on it, the marjorams took over! But I didn't mind because of the sheer numbers of insects that crowded around its flowers. As I walk past this border in summer, great clouds of bees, hoverflies and butterflies take to the air before settling again once I've passed. It's quite an experience.

With its abundance of purple flowers, marjoram is a feast of nectar. I used to have a National Collection of *Origanum* and would often explain the confusion between marjoram and oregano. Wild marjoram is the UK native, growing on the edge of woodland or on hedge banks, especially on alkaline soils. Because it is a wildflower, it's the caterpillar food plant for several moths including Burnished Brass and Green Carpet. Called oregano in Europe, the flavour of the dried herb comes from the soils and heat of the Mediterranean. Confusingly, what we buy as marjoram for cooking is the dried leaves of an annual plant, sweet marjoram, *Origanum majorana*. Also known as knotted marjoram, it packs an amazing flavour and it's really worth growing.

For a continuous supply of leaves for cooking, cut the stems to the base a couple of times during the growing year. It will spring back up again quickly, but if you leave it to flower, it's a major insect plant as well as looking beautiful.

Michaelmas daisies

Late season in my garden is a riot of colour with great swathes of asters standing tall at the back. Purple, mauve, pink or lavender blue, they peak around September, the open daisy flowers with golden centres drawing in huge numbers of insects including bees and hoverflies. They've been grown in cottage gardens because of ease of propagating and their spreading habit, lack of fussiness when it comes to soil and bright colours. They also work well, though, in contemporary designs or combined naturalistically with grasses in prairie planting. They range in height from plants growing above my head to compact types for rock gardens. Botanists have recently split them into several different genera, but gardeners still refer to them as asters!

There are hundreds of aster varieties and not all are the same when it comes to wildlife. A study that looked at the National Collection of asters showed that varieties varied greatly in their attractiveness to flower-visiting insects. It's worth observing plants for sale and noticing what insects are attracted to the flowers. I find that it's the old-fashioned varieties like the tall purple asters of my childhood, probably *Aster novae-angliae*, that are most crowded with butterflies in early autumn. Aster means 'star', which is descriptive, but its new name is *Symphyotrichum novae-angliae!* As a good source of nectar, they are loved by Red Admirals, Commas, Peacocks and Small Tortoiseshells, giving them a chance to stock up on food before autumn.

Nasturtium, *Tropaeolum majus*

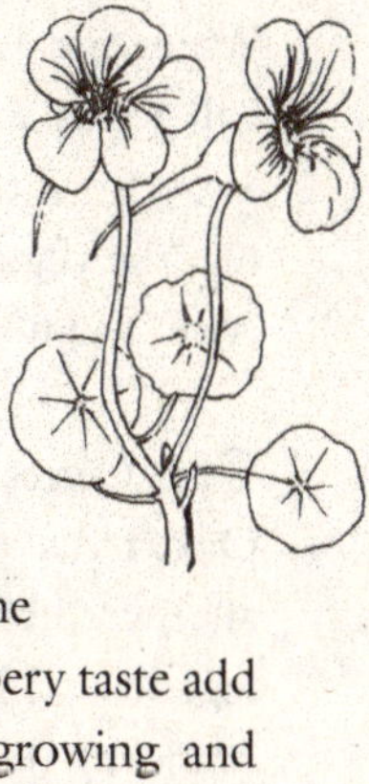

Those nasturtiums of my childhood left an indelible memory and I have grown them in every garden that I have made. Each year, I experiment with different colours, favourites being the soft creamy 'Milkmaid', the crimson 'Empress of India' and the deep red, almost black 'Black Velvet'. They are so easy to grow, either in the ground or in containers, and the leaves and edible flowers with their peppery taste add zing to salads. Because they're quick-growing and the large seeds are easy to handle, they encourage children to get into gardening. The more compact varieties can be used for hanging baskets.

There is a delightful climbing nasturtium called Canary creeper, *Tropaeolum peregrinum*, fast-growing with a mass of small fringed yellow flowers. Also an annual, this can be used to scramble up an archway in the vegetable garden, perhaps sharing the space with Spanish flag or Chilean glory flower.

These are annuals that, along with echiums, poppies, candytuft and cosmos, we grow around the vegetable garden where they bring in beneficial insects such as hoverflies. The nasturtiums are used for salads, but I'm fine with the leaves being shredded by caterpillars as well. As well as Garden Carpet moths, they are the larval food plant for three British butterflies: Green-veined White, Small White and Large White. Hopefully the nasturtiums will act as sacrificial plants, keeping the caterpillars away from the brassicas! But the best way to protect the vegetables without harming the insects is to cover them with fine netting.

Oak, *Quercus* spp

Oak trees are well known for being home to an incredibly wide range of wildlife. Steeped in legend and in history, the oak tree, with its leaves, branches, hollows and dead wood, is a sanctuary for bats, birds, mammals, lichens and fungi, and it's essential for some of our butterflies and moths. The caterpillars of the Purple Hairstreak butterfly feed exclusively on the leaves and flower buds of our two native species, sessile oak and pedunculate oak, as well as the introduced Turkey and Evergreen oaks. The adult butterflies are not easy to spot and you need to look up at the trees on a warm evening where they chase each other through the canopy. You are most likely to see them in broadleaved woodlands with mature trees, but this can include city parks where there are oaks. The males are a gorgeous dusky purple, the females have a couple of purple flashes on each forewing.

Oak Lutestring moths, *Cymatophorima diluta*, also feed on native oaks but, despite its name, the caterpillars of the Oak Eggar moth, *Lasiocampa quercus*, will also feed on a wide variety of trees and shrubs as well as bramble and heather. The moth species supported by oak trees are so numerous that I can't mention them all here. Many are frequently found in light traps, the ubiquitous quakers, pugs and carpets.

Gathering acorns that had fallen onto a lane, I germinated them and grew them on, being able to plant them out a few years later with a great sense of satisfaction.

Phlox, *Phlox paniculata*

This is a wide-ranging genus of garden plants that includes creeping Alpine varieties, woodlanders and annuals, but it is the commonly grown upright perennials that are particularly good for insects. They are really useful plants in the border because they are easy to grow and hardy, plus they rarely need staking, making them low maintenance. They are lovely as cut flowers too. Phlox have been extensively bred and come in shades of purple, pink, blue, magenta, white and red, or in flowers with different-coloured centres. They are fragrant and long-flowering, and can be Chelsea chopped to stagger the season. Easy to propagate too, you can understand why they were so often grown in cottage gardens.

The only problem that you sometimes get with phlox is powdery mildew, which can happen when it's hot and humid. The best way to avoid this is by having good air circulation around the plant or to choose varieties such as 'Jeanna', 'Violet Flame' or 'Franz Schubert' that are known to be less susceptible.

With their longer petal tubes, these taller types of border phlox are nectar- and pollen-rich, and can only be fed from by insects with long tongues. The moths that might visit in the evening include Convolvulus Hawk-moth, which has an especially long proboscis or, by day, you might spot a Hummingbird Hawk-moth hovering in front of a phlox flower to sip the nectar.

Primrose, *Primula vulgaris*; Cowslip, *Primula veris*

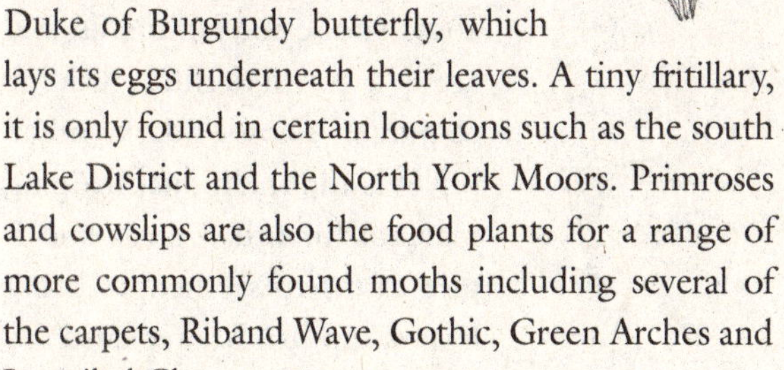

Of all the self-seeders in my garden, the flowers that are allowed to put themselves wherever they like are the cowslips and primroses. They pop up in unexpected places, delighting me with their freedom and spontaneity. Both are food plants for the rare Duke of Burgundy butterfly, which lays its eggs underneath their leaves. A tiny fritillary, it is only found in certain locations such as the south Lake District and the North York Moors. Primroses and cowslips are also the food plants for a range of more commonly found moths including several of the carpets, Riband Wave, Gothic, Green Arches and Ingrailed Clay.

Primroses have open pale yellow flowers with deep yellow centres, beautiful in the simplicity of their shapes. Cowslips have longer tubes and are a richer buttery yellow, and where they grow together, you can get a hybrid, the false oxlip. Both these lovely early spring flowers are native plants, primroses growing in woodland clearings, under hedges or on banks, and cowslips also growing in open meadows and downland. They're very easy to grow in gardens, existing happily in grass, on slopes and in flower borders.

They are easy to split, and this is best done just after flowering. They can be pulled apart into separate plantlets and planted in moisture-retentive soil. Bulking up quickly, they can then be divided again in a couple of years' time. This way, you can spread them across the garden for their cheerful spring flowers.

Privet, *Ligustrum vulgare*

Hedges give privacy to a garden, absorb noise and pollutants, and are a wonderful wildlife resource. Glossy, dark green privet is the traditional hedging material for urban areas and it grieves me to see hedges being ripped up to be replaced by fences. The dense foliage and fast growth rate of privet, together with its adaptability to different soils and growing conditions, made it popular. This is where sparrows would gather in flocks to chatter, a place of refuge and full of nest sites.

Privet can be trimmed into any height of hedge and can even be cut back hard to restore one that is overgrown and neglected. There are two types of privet: wild privet, *Ligustrum vulgare*, and garden privet, *Ligustrum ovalifolium*, which, as the name suggests, has more oval-shaped leaves than the wild. They have flowers for pollinators, berries for thrushes, and the leaves, especially of wild privet, are the food plant of the wonderful bright green and chunky Privet Hawk-moth caterpillars, despite them being poisonous to many other forms of life.

If you can't plant a hedge, a shrub of wild privet might help to entice a spectacular hawk-moth to your garden. The Privet Hawk-moth will come to light traps, and with its pink-and-black-striped body and wide wingspan, it is truly magnificent. The Eyed Hawk-moth and the Death's-head Hawk-moth, two other impressive beasts, use privet as a larval food plant, as do other beauties: Waved Umber, Copper Underwing, Lilac Beauty, Magpie and Swallow-tailed Moth.

Ragged robin, *Lychnis flos-cuculi*

One of the seventy or so wildflowers that I mingle among cultivated plants in my garden, ragged robin is fragile looking and graceful, but tough and hardy. I started it out in my small meadow where it happily grew in the damp soil among grasses before I

decided to experiment with it in the flower garden. It proved to be well-behaved enough, self-seeding freely but each plant making a neat basal rosette while sending up fine stems topped with fringed pink flowers. It's one of those plants that never impinges too much on its neighbours, so it forms an amicable community with hardy geraniums, verbascums, astrantias and aquilegias. The related red campion makes a much larger plant and needs a bit more careful planting, or it can overwhelm and shade out others.

Ragged robin is a good plant to grow around the edge of a pond where it will attract butterflies, bees and dragonflies, and birds will pick at its seeds. I've also found that it will grow successfully in the sun even where it's not so damp. It flowers at the time when cuckoos are calling, hence the species name of flos-cuculi. As well as providing nectar for adults, it is the food plant for caterpillars of several moths: Marbled Coronet, The Rivulet, The Campion and The Lychnis. Lychnis is the generic name for both the plant and the moth, and The Campion moth feeds on both ragged robin and red campion.

Roses, *Rosa* sp.

When I was growing up, it was common for gardeners to spray their roses throughout the season, killing any form of wildlife that might eat them. With increased awareness of the vulnerability of our insect life, this attitude has changed and many now don't resort to chemical sprays. In my organic garden, the leaves of roses are notched in the crisp circles made by female leaf cutting bees. These delightful little dark brown bees are solitary and they use the leaves to construct nest cells. One year, a female made her nest in the keyhole of our front door so we had to use another door instead!

Roses are the host plant for numerous beautiful moths, wonderfully patterned and colourful species such as Jersey Tiger, Elephant Hawk-moth and Green-brindled Crescent. There's the Garden Rose Tortrix, *Acleris variegana*, which sometimes comes to my light trap, and several other micro-moths, especially attracted to wild roses such as the dog rose. The larvae of the prettily marked Shoulder Stripe, *Earophila badiata*, also feed on the leaves of wild roses, and these can be grown in a mixed hedge where their hips provide food for thrushes, blackbirds and redwings.

The open shape of single varieties or semi-doubles are best for insects. Roses don't produce nectar but they do have protein-rich pollen, which bees need for energy and for development of their brood. And aphids, rather than being seen as a problem, are food for ladybirds, lacewings and other natural predators.

Sedums

In early autumn, the central path in my garden is edged either side with sedums. It marks a spectacular moment and provides a huge source of nectar en masse for a great variety of butterflies, bumblebees, hoverflies and true flies. On a warm day, when the nectar is in full flow, it's an incredible experience to walk down between the two rows of plants, insects flying up all the way along. And it was deliberately planted that way for that thrill.

These are all plants of what used to be called *Sedum spectabile*, and although they have been renamed as *Hylotelephium*, I still think of them as sedums. The other common name is ice plant. With their pink-purple flowers arranged in flat heads, they make a suitable landing pad for insects, which can then crawl over the surface feeding from each individual star-shaped flower. Just as with umbellifers, they are crowded with flowers, which means that insects don't have to keep travelling between plants, saving energy. They can feed up before autumn, and garden butterflies – Red Admiral, Small Tortoiseshell, Peacock, Comma – are constant visitors. Also by day, the honey-scented flowers are a magnet for Silver Y moths.

Sedums have fleshy, succulent leaves that can store water, making them useful for resisting drought. If you grow them in rich soil, their growth means they can flop. The best way around this is to grow them hard, not feeding them so that they stay in nice tight clumps.

Sweet rocket, *Hesperis matronalis*

Sweet rocket, also known as dame's violet, is one of those plants that I wouldn't be without. Its colour varies from deep purple through pale lilac to white, but it is the white variety that I let seed in great drifts through my borders. Held on tall stems, the flowers seem to float cloud-like in the air, especially when backlit by evening light, a visionary moment. And it's in the evening that they give off their sweet perfume.

Moths and butterflies feed from the flowers, as do bees and hoverflies, but it's also valuable as a caterpillar plant, food for Green-veined White and Orange-tip butterfly larvae. I've watched Orange-tip butterflies mating on the flowerheads and later seen their green caterpillars feasting on the long thin seedpods.

Sweet rocket often grows in great abundance in all its colourways alongside rivers where it likes the moist soil, but it's versatile enough to grow almost anywhere. As a biennial, it will flower in the spring after it is sown, but it seeds freely and, once you get your eye in for young plants, you can make choices about where to leave them be or to take them out. As well as the sweetness of its evening scent, sweet rocket brings a naturalistic, loose feeling to the garden. Double-flowering forms, however, need to be propagated by cuttings. I pick sweet rocket for the house, mixing its sweetly scented flowers into bunches of alliums, irises, aquilegias and deep burgundy cirsium thistles.

Tobacco plant, *Nicotiana alata*

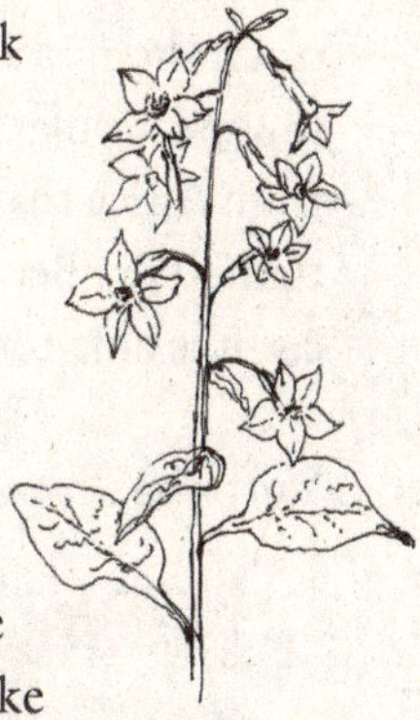

The more variety that you can pack into your garden, the better. From trees and shrubs with perennials, bulbs, grasses and annuals, you will provide numerous niches for shelter and food for wildlife. Annuals and bedding plants have a high ratio of flower to foliage, bringing wonderful colour to the garden. But the choices that we make in a garden centre can really impact on insect life, and some popular bedding plants such as begonias have no nectar. Instead we can choose single dahlias, salvias, scabious, cosmos, alyssum, bidens, and many others.

Tobacco plants give off their perfume at night, the species *Nicotiana alata* being the best because some modern varieties have less scent. A single seed packet of *Nicotiana* 'Sensation Mixed' will give a range of colours from white through pale pink to cerise and, as well as flowering in the day, be a heady delight in the dusk. The flowers form a tube that opens out into a star shape, and you can grow tobacco plants in borders, by patios or in containers.

The tallest species that is commonly grown is *Nicotiana sylvestris,* and this is a statuesque and beautiful plant. It has very long white tubular flowers, which are too deep for our native moths to reach the nectar, but by growing it you may attract the spectacular *Convolvulus* Hawk-moth, a migrant from Africa that is becoming a more frequent visitor to the UK. Because it has an unusually long proboscis, it is able to feed on flowers with long tubes.

Verbena, *Verbena bonariensis*

A plant that has become very popular in recent years is this lovely verbena, sometimes known as purple-top vervain. Much used in designs at the Chelsea Flower Show, it can now be found everywhere, and for good reason. It has a very long flowering period, starting in early summer and continuing right through to autumn. It's a tall plant yet it retains an airy openness thanks to its straight stems and branching flower tops. This means that you can place it at the front of the border and still see through it. It combines beautifully with grasses, making it suitable for both traditional and contemporary gardens. And above all, it is excellent for insects.

The purple of verbena has a day-glow, vivid quality that makes it really stand out. Its numerous small nectar-rich flowers attract bees, hoverflies, butterflies and moths, later having seed for birds. Because it flowers well into autumn, it helps sustain insects in late season. In my last garden, I grew verbena in huge blocks for the dramatic impact of massed purple. Now living in a frost hollow, I give it protection by letting it seed in the gaps between the paving stones of the terrace. These create just enough of a microclimate for the plants to survive the winter, and I love the effect of the flowers floating at head height.

Butterflies are attracted to verbena, especially in years when there's an influx of Painted Ladies, and Hummingbird Hawk-moths, migrated from the Mediterranean, love to feed from its tubular flowers.

Violet, *Viola spp.*

Although I'm unlikely to see them in my garden and in many other people's, violets are essential food plants for some of our most threatened butterflies, Pearl-bordered and Small Pearl-bordered fritillaries. Dog violets grow in woodland clearings, benefiting from coppicing that brings openness and light, and have suffered from a loss of habitat. Who knows what effect it could have if large swathes of

British gardens contained these food plants?

It is the caterpillars of fritillaries especially that need the leaves of species of violet, common dog violet, marsh violet, sweet violet and wild pansy. But these lovely wildflowers also host moths: Broad-bordered Yellow Underwing, Plain Wave, Ingrailed Clay and Clouded Buff.

Wild pansy has been grown in UK gardens for centuries. Also known as heartsease, it was used as the love potion in *A Midsummer Night's Dream*, creating chaos, and, in Shakespeare's lines, named 'love-in-idleness'. Quirky vernacular names include tickle-my-fancy, Jack-jump-up-and-kiss-me and come-and-cuddle-me. With its bonny face and three colours – purple, cream and yellow – heartsease has long been a favourite of cottage gardens.

For scent, you need to grow sweet violet, *Viola odorata*, a deep blue flower, sometimes white, with an intense perfume. You need to really appreciate the first sniff of its flowers because olfactory fatigue means you stop smelling it for a while after that. Woodland plants, they need to be grown out of full sun, so I have mine planted beneath some hostas. Dog violets look similar but they are a bit paler and are unscented.

Wallflower, *Erysimum* 'Bowle's Mauve'

Wallflowers are a popular bedding plant, grown for their sumptuous colours and rich perfume. They are, however, biennial, grown from seed in late spring, planted out in autumn and flowering in spring at the same time as tulips – a classic combination. There is also this perennial wallflower, a small bush with grey-green leaves and deep mauve flowers that continue for months on end. It's invaluable for its lovely colour, good as a cut flower and very attractive to insects.

As the flowers open, the stems keep lengthening in a long progression of blooms. I prune them back to leaves and side shoots once they start to look less showy so other stems will flower, and this helps to keep the plants compact. Perennial wallflowers are usually considered short-term, but I've had some that have lasted for five years. Others have succumbed to the winter after just one year, but they are easy to strike from cuttings, and it is worth having some in reserve.

These are plants that fit the cottage garden look but also fit well with urban and contemporary garden style, combining beautifully with ornamental grasses. Pollinating insects include bees, moths, hoverflies and butterflies, especially Small Tortoiseshell. I grow 'Bowle's Mauve' in pots to either side of the front door, and if there's one plant that will attract a Hummingbird Hawk-moth, it's this. That's a magic moment, the bird-like blur, the flash of orange hindwings, the long proboscis feeding from the purple flowers.

Willowherbs, *Epilobium* sp.

The larvae of some of our loveliest moths feed on willowherbs, plants that many gardeners spend time ejecting from their gardens! The hoary willowherb, *Epilobium parviflorum*, is the small species with rather insignificant pale pink flowers that eagerly seeds itself among borders. Rosebay willowherb is the giant, a successful coloniser of railway lines and waste ground, also known as fireweed for taking advantage of burnt ground. That gave it its other name of bombweed as it flourished in city bombsites after the blitz.

Rosebay willowherb, *Chamaenerion angustifolium*, is the host plant for two very beautiful moths, the Elephant Hawk-moth and the Small Elephant

Hawk-moth. It's a beautiful plant and if it wasn't so invasive, gardeners would be desperate to grow it. Growing to over two metres, it has graceful purple-pink flower spikes and, as the name suggests, willow-like slender leaves. The seed pods open on warm days, sending clouds of tiny downy seeds to settle in new places, one of the reasons it gets drawn along the corridor of railways by the draught created by trains.

Rather than grow the species, I planted white rosebay willowherb, which stands serene and tall at the back of the border. It still needs careful controlling or it will ebb out and clash with other plants, but it's worth it for its grace and beauty, and the moths that find their way into my light trap: not only the fabulous hawk-moths but also Small Angle Shades, carpet moths and Setaceous Hebrew Character.

Yarrow *Achillea* spp and cultivars

One of the pretty little moths that I might disturb when I'm gardening is the Yarrow Plume, *Gillmeria pallidactyla*. This is a micro-moth so it's not a big showy species, but it has a subtle charm. It's not surprising that I see it because I grow both common yarrow, *Achillea millefolium*, and sneeze-wort, *Achillea ptarmica*, in my small garden meadow, as well as colourful garden varieties of yarrow in the borders. Yarrow Plume has narrow wings that are biscuit-coloured with wedge-shaped ends and could easily be overlooked.

It's just one of the moths that feed on yarrow, others being Ruby Tiger, Mottled Beauty, Yarrow Pug and Mullein Wave.

Yarrow is a strong growing plant, a native for meadows and a good source of nectar for bees. Its white flowers are arranged in a flat top, clustered together, tinged pink as they fade. The leaves have a medicinal scent and look ferny and feathery – millefolium means 1000 leaves. This is a very adaptable plant capable of growing in different types of soil, and has been bred for a wide variety of colours: pink, apricot, orange, yellow and ruby red. Drought tolerant, it can also easily cope with wet soils, making this a very resilient plant.

The tallest cultivar is a striking plant called 'Coronation gold'. It has silvery-grey foliage and bright golden flowers that are good for cutting and air drying, hanging upside down to preserve them for winter decoration.

7

Notes and Resources

Further reading and resources:

Book list

Crafer, Tim: *Foodplant List for the Caterpillars of Britain's Butterflies and Larger Moths* (Atropos Publishing 2005)

Fry, Reg and Waring, Paul: *A Guide to Moth Traps and their Use* (third edition) (Amateur Entomologist's Society, 2020)

Henwood, Barry and Sterling, Phil: *Field Guide to the Caterpillars of Great Britain and Ireland* Illustrated by Richard Lewington (Bloomsbury 2020)

Manley, Chris: *British & Irish Moths: A Photographic Guide* (third edition) (Bloomsbury Wildlife, 2021)

Newland, David; Still, Robert and Swash, Andy: *Britain's Day-flying Moths* (second edition) (Princeton University Press, 2019)

Niemann, Derek: *RSPB First Book of Butterflies and Moths* (RSPB, 2012)

RSPB: *Foldout RSPB ID Spotlight Moths* Illustrated by Richard Lewington (RSPB)

Sterling, Phil and Parson, Mark: *Field Guide to the Micro-moths of Great Britain and Ireland* (second edition) Illustrated by Richard Lewington (Bloomsbury 2023)

Townsend, Martin and Waring, Paul: *Concise Guide to the Moths of Great Britain and Ireland* (second edition)

Illustrated by Richard Lewington (Bloomsbury Wildlife 2019)

Waring, Paul and Townsend, Martin: *Field Guide to the Moths of Great Britain and Ireland* (third edition) Illustrated by Richard Lewington, (Bloomsbury 2018)

Useful information

Moth Night is an annual celebration of moth recording throughout Britain and Ireland by moth recording enthusiasts. It is organised by Atropos, Butterfly Conservation and the UK Centre for Ecology and Hydrology.

Garden Moth Scheme The GMS collects data from The United Kingdom, The Republic of Ireland and the Channel Islands and now contains well over 1 million records, making it a valuable resource. The website has a list of contacts for each region if you're interested in taking part. For anyone who is interested in moths, the newsletters alone give a fascinating insight into what is happening in the moth world. There are also links to the Facebook group, and this is a great way to have help with identification. gardenmothscheme.org.uk .

Butterfly Conservation is the UK charity dedicated to saving butterflies and moths. It manages over thirty nature reserves, gives advice to landowners and managers on how to conserve and restore habitats, and has an excellent website – butterfly-conservation.org – that includes an illustrated A-Z of moths and butterflies with details of habitat, distribution and caterpillar food plants.

UK Moths is an online guide to the moths of Britain and Ireland with excellent photography and a section on moths by family, which helps to narrow down an identification.

The binoculars that I mentioned are Pentax 'Papilio', which are able to close focus and reveal the fascinating detail of insects but also spot them from further away.

The brilliant **Anglian Lepidopterist Supplies** is a family business in Norfolk that sells everything you need to start trapping from traps to pots, pheromones to nets and magnifying lenses as well as bat detectors.

Atropos is a journal for butterfly, moth and dragonfly enthusiasts, and they have a mail order service Atropos Books.

List of butterflies and moths mentioned in this book

Common name	Species name
Adonis Blue	*Polyommatus bellargus*
Angle Shades	*Phlogophora meticulosa*
Antler Moth	*Cerapteryx graminis*
Beautiful Golden Y	*Autographa pulchrina*
Bedstraw Hawk-moth	*Hyles gallii*
Bird-cherry Ermine moth	*Yponomeuta evonymella*
Box moth	*Cydalima perspectalis*
Brimstone	*Gonepteryx rhamni*
Brimstone Moth	*Opisthograptis luteolata*
Broad-Bordered Bee Hawk-moth	*Hemaris fuciformis*
Broad-bordered Yellow Underwing	*Noctua fimbriata*
Brown Hairstreak	*Thecla betulae*
Buff Ermine	*Spilosoma lutea*
Buff-tip	*Phalera bucephala*
Burnished Brass	*Diachrysia chrysitis*
Buttoned Snout	*Hypena rostralis*
Chimney Sweeper	*Odezia atrata*
Chinese Character	*Cilix glaucata*
Clouded Buff	*Diacrisia sannio*
Clouded Yellow	*Gonepteryx rhamni*
Comma	*Polygonia c-album*

Common Blue	*Polyommatus icarus*
Common Footman	*Eilema lurideola*
Common Heath	*Ematurga atomaria*
Common Quaker	*Orthosia cerasi*
Convolvulus Hawk-moth	*Agrius convolvuli*
Copper Underwing	*Amphipyra pyramidea*
Coxcomb Prominent	*Ptilodon capucina*
Currant Pug	*Eupithecia assimilata*
Death's-head Hawk-moth	*Acherontia atropos*
December Moth	*Poecilocampa populi*
Duke of Burgundy	*Hamearis lucina*
Elephant Hawk-moth	*Deilephila elpenor*
Emperor Moth	*Saturnia pavonia*
Eyed Hawk-moth	*Smerinthus ocellata*
Flame Shoulder	*Ochropleura plecta*
Foxglove Pug	*Eupithecia pulchellata*
Frosted Orange	*Gortyna flavago*
Garden Pebble	*Evergestis forficalis*
Garden Rose Tortrix	*Acleris variegana*
Gatekeeper	*Pyronia tithonus*
Ghost Moth	*Hepialus humuli*
Goat Moth	*Cossus cossus*
Grass Eggar	*Lasiocampa trifolii*
Green Carpet	*Colostygia pectinataria*
Green-brindled Crescent	*Allophyes oxyacanthae*
Green-veined White	*Pieris napi*

Hebrew Character	*Orthosia gothica*
Holly Blue	*Celastrina argiolus*
Hornet Moth	*Sesia apiformis*
Ingrailed Clay	*Diarsia mendica*
Jersey Tiger	*Euplagia quadripunctaria*
Kentish Glory	*Endromis versicolora*
Large Emerald	*Geometra papilionaria*
Large White	*Pieris brassicae*
Large Yellow Underwing	*Noctua pronuba*
Latticed Heath	*Chiasmia clathrata*
Leopard Moth	*Zeuzera pyrina*
Lesser Yellow Underwing	*Noctua comes*
Lilac Beauty	*Apeira syringaria*
Lobster Moth	*Stauropus fagi*
Lunar Yellow Underwing	*Noctua orbona*
Magpie	*Abraxas grossulariata*
Map-winged Swift	*Korscheltellus fusconebulosa*
Marbled Coronet	*Hadena confusa*
Marbled White	*Melanargia galathea*
Meadow Brown	*Maniola jurtina*
Merveille du Jour	*Griposia aprilina*
Mint moth	*Pyrausta aurata*
Mother of Pearl	*Patania ruralis*
Mother Shipton	*Callistege mi*
Mottled Beauty	*Alcis repandata*
Mullein moth	*Cucullia verbasci*

Mullein Wave	*Scopula marginepunctata*
Oak Eggar	*Lasiocampa quercus*
Oak Lutestring	*Cymatophorima diluta*
Oak Processionary Moth	*Thaumetopoea processionea*
Old Lady Moth	*Morma mauro*
Orange-tip	*Anthocharis cardamines*
Painted Lady	*Vanessa cardui*
Pale Tussock	*Calliteara pudibunda*
Peacock	*Aglais io*
Pearl-bordered Fritillary	*Boloria euphrosyne*
Peppered Moth	*Biston betularia*
Plain Wave	*Idaea straminata*
Poplar Hawk-moth	*Laothoe populi*
Powdered Quaker	*Orthosia gracilis*
Privet Hawk-moth	*Sphinx ligustri*
Purple Clay	*Diarsia brunnea*
Purple Hairstreak	*Favonius quercus*
Purple Thorn	*Selenia tetralunaria*
Puss Moth	*Cerura vinula*
Red Admiral	*Vanessa atalanta*
Red Sword-grass	*Xylena vetusta*
Ringlet	*Aphantopus hyperantus*
Ruby Tiger	*Phragmatobia fuliginosa*
Satellite	*Eupsilia transversa*
Scalloped Hazel	*Odontopera bidentata*
Scalloped Oak	*Crocallis elinguaria*

Scotch Argus	*Erebia aethiops*
Setaceous Hebrew Character	*Xestia c-nigrum*
Shoulder Stripe	*Earophila badiata*
Silver Y	*Autographa gamma*
Silver-striped Hawk-moth	*Hippotion celerio*
Silver-studded Blue	*Plebejus argus*
Six-spot Burnet	*Zygaena filipendulae*
Slender Brindle	*Apamea scolopacina*
Small Angle Shades	*Euplexia lucipara*
Small Copper	*Lycaena phlaeas*
Small Heath	*Coenonympha pamphilus*
Small Magpie	*Anania hortulata*
Small Pearl-bordered Fritillary	*Boloria selene*
Small Tortoiseshell	*Aglais urticae*
Small White	*Pieris rapae*
Snout	*Hypena proboscidalis*
Speckled Wood	*Pararge aegeria*
Spectacle	*Abrostola tripartita*
Striped Hawk-moth	*Hyles livornica*
Swallow-tailed Moth	*Ourapteryx sambucaria*
The Campion	*Sideridis rivularis*
The Herald	*Scoliopteryx libatrix*
The Lychnis	*Hadena bicruris*
The Rivulet	*Perizoma affinitata*
Tiger Moth	*Arctia caja*

True Lover's Knot	*Lycophotia porphyrea*
Twin-spotted Quaker	*Anorthoa munda*
Vapourer	*Orgyia antiqua*
Wall	*Lasiommata megera*
Waved Umber	*Menophra abruptaria*
Winter Moth	*Operophtera brumata*
Yarrow Plume	*Gillmeria pallidactyla*
Yarrow Pug	*Eupithecia millefoliata*

A word on the illustrations

I really enjoyed making the ink drawings of butterflies, moths and plants – but please bear in mind that these are illustrations and may not be entirely botanically or scientifically accurate. While I hope you will find them useful, they may not be sufficient for identifying purposes. It is always advisable to refer to specialist guides when identifying species you are not familiar with.

Acknowledgements

I'd like to say thank you to Dave Grundy for getting me interested in moth trapping in the first place. Special thanks go to Mike Cook, the Garden Moth Scheme coordinator for North East England, for his help over the years with identification, his fact-filled and interesting newsletters and for checking through the text of this book. I'm very grateful to Sara Hunt of Saraband for asking me to write about one of my favourite subjects, and for being such a supportive and friendly publisher.

The Author

Susie White is a gardening and travel writer, broadcaster, wildlife photographer and lecturer. With a lifelong love of gardening, she has written several books on the subject and is a regular contributor to *The English Garden, Garden Design Journal, BBC Countryfile* and *The Guardian's* Country Diary, and she has been the garden columnist for *My Weekly* magazine since 2014. She is the designer of classic English gardens in the UK and in Sweden. Her own garden, created from scratch in a north Pennine valley, blends wildflowers with cultivated plants and is a magnet for wildlife. It was featured on BBC *Gardeners' World* and in Clive Nichol's book *Brilliant English Gardens* and in *Gardens Illustrated*. The author of *Second Nature* (2024), her forthcoming title for the In the Moment series is *Nature's Almanac: A Gift for Every Day of the Year*. Susie combines her gardening and writing with painting, drawing, photography and pottery.

In the Moment series: related titles

Further titles in this series on wildlife and on earth-friendly gardening practices include these below.

Insects

The Butterfly
Nigel Andrew

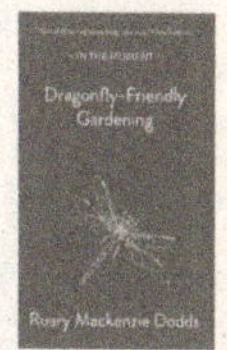

Dragonfly-Friendly Gardening
Ruary Mackenzie Dodds

Gardening and the Natural World

Permaculture
Maya Blackwell

Watching Wildlife
Jim Crumley

Dark Skies
Anna Levin

Nature's Almanac
Susie White
(coming soon)